FASHION MADE FAIR

FASHION MADE FAIR

MODERN · INNOVATIVE · SUSTAINABLE

ELLEN KÖHRER

MAGDALENA SCHAFFRIN

PRESTEL

MUNICH · LONDON · NEW YORK

CONTENTS

INTRODUCTION

"It's just fashion. Innovative, desirable and responsibly produced," is how Bruno Pieters describes his brand Honest By. In doing so he is accurately reflecting the spirit of the times. So this quote has become the core message of this book. Fashion is a mirror of our society, in all its facets. Increasing numbers of fashion brands all around the globe are designing modern, cool, elegant fashion that makes sense. You cannot see immediately that it has been manufactured in a fair manner which is not only environmentally friendly but also makes sparing use of resources. It is simply fashion, as Pieters observed. And precisely this fashion is what we are presenting in FASHION MADE FAIR. Looking at the generous photo sections you will see that fashion can be luxurious, minimalist or casual. The portraits and stories of the labels and brands clearly demonstrate what makes it so unusual. These pioneers of the fashion sector show how we shall dress in future, with responsibly produced clothing which respects both people and the environment.

This type of fashion is still searching for a name with an attractive ring to it. Descriptions like sustainable fashion, green fashion, ethical fashion, eco-fair fashion or slow fashion stamp it in a way that most designers neither want nor appreciate. Because all too often it is associated with something unfashionable or old-fashioned – ecological fashion from the Germany of the 1970s and 1980s, shapeless clothing made of jute or hemp. Some forty years have passed since the beginnings of green fashion; in the meantime, style and design have adapted to the spirit of the times and look no different from ordinary fashion. Designers have understood that fashion is what stands in the foreground and that stories about the social and ecological commitment of their brands will at most serve to explain their collections better.

But what is it, then, that distinguishes this type of fashion from ordinary fashion? It expresses a higher claim to quality than mere clothing as a product does. It is a claim to quality that goes beyond the material, processing and design of clothing, shoes and accessories, a claim that includes values. A claim that these products will damage neither the environment nor people, and that ideally they will even serve them. And so the expression "sustainable fashion" will always contain an ecological and social dimension. Transparency is a third, important pillar in the self-understanding of designers and brands, because transparency evokes trust. Those who work in a transparent way cannot and do not want to hide anything.

Sustainability in fashion is a very complex subject with many sides to it, since it refers to the entire product cycle. In the case of a T-shirt, for example, it extends from the cultivation of the cotton to the manufacture of the fabric, the sewing of the T-shirt and the transport from the clothing factory to the shops; and then the way it is cared for by its owner and even its disposal. Production includes social aspects like humane working conditions and fair pay for workers, from the farmers in the fields to the seamstress in the clothing factory.

And at the same time ecological aspects also play an important role; the textile industry is considered one of the most damaging industries worldwide with regard to the environment. And so the biological cultivation of natural fibres, the recycling of materials to make new fibres and fabrics, and the avoidance of damaging chemicals in production are all essential. Once the fashion reaches the shops, consumers are also involved in the decisions as to what will be sold successfully. Consumers have more influence than they realise. They can help to ensure that fashion as a whole becomes more sustainable and that we purchase less clothing of higher quality and do not succumb to every fast fashion bargain. In line with Vivienne Westwood's motto: "Buy less, choose well, make it last."

In FASHION MADE FAIR we are taking a look behind the scenes of the fashion sector. We want to remove prejudices; that is why we have written this book. We, that is the authors Ellen Köhrer and Magdalena Schaffrin. Köhrer is a journalist, writer and blogger; for years she has written for newspapers and magazines. Her blog Grünistdasneueschwarz.de focuses on eco-fair fashion. She presents portraits of designers, analyses the business models of innovative fashion brands and researches in the textile factories of Asia. Her co-author Schaffrin is a fashion designer who has specialised in sustainable fashion since completing her studies. She is the co-founder of Greenshowroom, the first green luxury fashion fair held during Berlin Fashion Week. As an expert on sustainable fashion she also works as a lecturer and speaker and advises companies in the selection and marketing of sustainable fashion brands.

We met during an interview at Fashion Week. Nine months later we then agreed to meet on a sunny afternoon in April 2014, to exchange ideas during a walk together along the Landwehr Canal in Kreuzberg in Berlin; Schaffrin's nine-month-old son accompanied us in his pram. We soon came to the conclusion that we knew of no attractive, positive, lavishly illustrated book about sustainable fashion and that we already had an idea what one might look like. Independently from each other we had both already played with the idea of producing a fashion book of that kind. So why not do so together? No sooner said than done. We set to work to develop the concept, went in search of a publisher and started on our research.

In FASHION MADE FAIR we introduce selected designers and brands who have impressed us with their collections, concepts and stories. The selection was not easy. In the end we chose thirty-three fashion brands from Europe, the United States, New Zealand and Bangladesh who convinced us stylistically and who scored with fresh ideas, new design approaches and innovative strategies. They included small labels as well as major brands.

FASHION MADE FAIR presents portraits of fashion brands which by virtue of their choice of materials have made a decision in favour of better working conditions and environmental protection. They include brands like Vivienne Westwood, who has bags made by hand in Africa, thereby providing local people with jobs and prospects. Or Patagonia, which with its unusual advertising campaigns encourages its customers to an increased awareness in choosing outdoor clothing of high quality and with a long useful life.

Hessnatur, a German pioneer of sustainable fashion, supports the cultivation of the indigo plant to dye fabric in Bangladesh, manufacturing locally and sharing its expertise with other producers.

We portray labels like Christopher Ræburn from London, who recycles parachutes, army clothing and lifeboats and uses them to make cool, new, robust clothing. Or the Danish knitwear label Aiayu, whose designer discovered in Bolivia that you can make exquisite pullovers from llama wool and who combines modern Danish design with this unusual material and traditional knitting art. And Mud Jeans from the Netherlands produces fairly manufactured jeans of organic cotton which customers can lease instead of buy, and then recycles them as new products such as pullovers or cardigans.

And we also spoke to six experts about different approaches which contribute to making the fashion industry more environmentally and socially aware. In our interview with Bruno Pieters the subject is the importance of transparency in fashion and his visions of the future. We spoke with Marie-Claire Daveu from the French luxury concern Kering Group about the importance of the carbon footprint in luxury fashion. Michael Braungart and Friederike von Wedel-Parlow explain the design concept of Cradle to Cradle and its importance for the fashion sector. Orsola de Castro, co-founder of the Fashion Revolution movement, focuses on the influence and power of the consumer. And finally Lily Cole speaks about slow fashion and her social company Impossible.

We wish you much pleasure in reading, leafing through and browsing in FASHION MADE FAIR.

ISABELL DE HILLERIN

BERLIN,
GERMANY

TRADITION MEETS MODERNITY

A visit to a workshop in the Neukölln district of Berlin: a bright shop and studio on a small, tree-lined canal with a large cutting table, beneath which Isabell de Hillerin's dog is lying peacefully. Elegant evening dresses in Bordeaux red, dark blue and black are hanging on a clothes stand; beside them are cream-coloured blazers in flowing fabrics. Isabell de Hillerin explains that an actress has just called for a fitting session. Only at second sight do we notice the loving attention to detail in the work: narrow macramé inserts, a hand-embroidered collar and epaulettes that recall starfish. Everything is very carefully matched, tone on tone.

Isabell de Hillerin had the idea of linking together tradition and modernity while studying for her master's degree in Fashion Design in Barcelona. After graduating in 2009 she moved to Berlin and founded her own label, which simply bears her name.

Looking back to her Romanian roots, de Hillerin travelled to the country of her ancestors in search of traditional fabrics and folk weaving techniques which are increasingly being forgotten. She found women in villages and little artisanal firms that still practise these old craft skills. She got them to show her the old patterns which were used either on clothing or on carpets and table runners. The designer reduced the colours, abstracted the patterns and had her designs executed by the women in Romania. "The result is something completely new that doesn't look like folklore," explains de Hillerin. It is also completely successful. Since then you will find these traditional elements in all her collections. In the meantime she has also added embroidery and handwoven fabrics from Moldavia. Her collections are produced entirely in Romania.

De Hillerin already has contacts in both countries who communicate with the craftswomen, take care of the logistics, travel to the women in the villages and ensure that delivery dates are adhered to.

De Hillerin named her Autumn/Winter 2015/16 collection "Să-l porți sănătoasă" after a Romanian proverb which, literally translated, means "Wear it in health." It is a wish expressed when a new item of clothing is purchased. "It means that you should enjoy wearing it and appreciate it," explains de Hillerin. An appealing thought that it is only too easy to comply with in the case of de Hillerin's elegantly cut fashion made with high-quality materials. A successful combination of tradition and modernity.

www.isabelldehillerin.com

HELLEN VAN REES

HENGELO,
NETHERLANDS

THE TWEED ARTIST

Hellen van Rees lays thread over thread in snaking lines on the paper pattern. Layer upon layer, colour upon colour. As in a painting. Then she joins the threads to create a tweed fabric using a kind of weaving technique that she developed while studying for her master's degree at Central Saint Martins College in London. She found her inspiration in Chanel's classic twinsets. "I was particularly fascinated by the wide range of different yarns, materials and surfaces which were woven together," says Hellen van Rees, who develops her own fabrics using remnants from Dutch yarn factories. Her preferred materials are cotton and wool. The threads with their different colours, strengths and surfaces give her handmade clothing its artistic structure and colour.

With this idea and her master's in her pocket van Rees returned to her native Holland in 2012 and founded her own business. Her very first collection caused a stir when Lady Gaga appeared in one of her grey tweed dresses decorated with cubes.

Van Rees's classic, simple designs are a new interpretation of Coco Chanel's fashions from the 1920s. That is intentional: "So much happens in the material that the cut must speak for itself." There are no leftover scraps of material or wasted fabric in van Rees's clothing, because instead of producing lengths of material in the usual way she produces her fabric in the shape of her tops, dresses and accessories and stitches the separate pieces together. This is haute couture on a small scale; each item of clothing is unique and has its own character, produced by hand with care and affection. "I like the lively character and uniqueness of hand-made fabrics; I find it much more interesting than machine-made material which always looks exactly the same." But this exclusivity has its price. Which is why nowadays van Rees has her tweed-like patterns printed on silk that she then uses to make more affordable clothing. Replicas of her own fabric art, so to speak. She also produces bags and shoes and home accessories such as cushions with her woven art. www.hellenvanrees.com

HELLEN *VAN* REES

Cuttheshades,
Spring/Summer 2015
(left page)

The Importance of Ideas
and Information,
Spring/Summer 2016
(right page)

Outoftheblue,
Autumn/Winter 2014/15
(page 16)

BRUNO PIETERS
ANTWERP, BELGIUM

A MODEL OF TRANSPARENCY

Antwerp, Bruno Pieters' atelier: a vast room with high ceilings and a white writing desk in the centre. On the floor stands a carton containing brightly coloured plastic items: a comb, a unicorn, a palm leaf the size of your hand and a sign bearing the message: "Revolution. honest by." Not a toy, but the designer's latest coup: the "Download EP01" collection. Accessories from the 3D printer, EP stands for "Easy Print." Pieters developed the idea together with the Spanish design collective Comme Des Machines. You can download the printing instructions from Pieters' website, including addresses listing where you can find the nearest 3D hub and a recommendation to use compostable or recycled plastic as filler material.

That is typical of Pieters. Environmentally conscious, a stickler for details and transparent. These are rare qualities in a sector in which people live from appearances and a curtain of silence is drawn over the conditions under which our clothing is manufactured. "For me, transparency is not a luxury; it is absolutely essential," observes Pieters.

Pieters knows exactly what he is talking about: he has worked for big brands like Christian Lacroix and Martin Margiela, and he was also the creative director of Hugo, Hugo Boss's avant-garde line. "When I was working for Boss, I believed I was working with the very best fabrics and materials – they came from suppliers who in some cases had existed for over a hundred years and with whom many other firms in the fashion industry also work." At the time Pieters was not aware that they did not take into account either fair working conditions or the environment.

After a sabbatical and journeys to India his worldview underwent a radical change. From that point onwards he started to think about the environment, animal protection and children's rights. Today his life credo is adapted from Gandhi: "Be the change you want to see in the world."

With this new life philosophy in mind, Pieters founded Honest By in 2012 as the first fashion brand in the world to be 100 per cent transparent. On his Internet platform he sells minimalist fashion for men and women that displays an architectural flair. The collections are created exclusively using certified materials such as organic cotton or organic silk. Today Pieters is a vegan and dispenses with the use of leather and fur.

In Honest By's online shop Pieters reveals his entire supply chain. You can read all the details regarding which materials have been used, from which suppliers they came and how they were manufactured. The calculation of prices is also detailed online, including Pieters' own markup. Pieters refuses to accept the arguments of fashion retailers who often say that complete transparency is impossible because the research is too expensive. "Everything is possible if customers demand it. Customers have much more power than they realise."
www.honestby.com

BRUNO PIETERS

"THE STORY BEHIND THE DESIGN NEEDS TO BE *AS* BE*A*UTIFUL *AS* THE DESIGN ITSELF"

Interview with fashion designer Bruno Pieters about transparency in fashion, how 3D design will revolutionise the whole fashion industry and about his visions of the future of fashion.

Bruno Pieters, Honest By is the first brand in the world to offer price transparency to customers and to make the entire supply chain public. Why do you do that?

Honest By is a brand that I wanted as a client. Because I was becoming aware that what brands are selling is not what customers are buying. They were selling us a dream but what we are buying is often a nightmare for thousands of other beings involved. With Honest By I want to give the customer all the information needed in order for them to be able to shop consciously. Most of the pieces in the Honest By collections are made out of certified organic or recycled materials. The origin and production process of those materials can be viewed by the client on our website. For certain items we were not able to publish and share the information with the consumer because our supplier asked us not to, but we were always given the information. Disclosing the price calculation was also very important to me – as this shows that every party involved was remunerated in a fair way. I believe if price transparency became an international law, issues such as child labour and other unethical practices could be detected easily and prevented. The 100 per cent transparency concept that I created

with Honest By was something that I wanted as a customer and as someone who loves fashion. I believe every individual needs to be able to access that information. Knowing exactly what we are buying is not a privilege; it is a necessity today. That level of transparency is crucial in order for us to be able to make choices that will protect our future and that of generations to come.

But how do you manage transparency in practical terms?

It took a team of five people one year to gather all the information we needed to have to be able to launch Honest By in 2012. We have spent most of our time finding new suppliers, doing background checks and researching them. It was a relatively small group of people who investigated every manufacturer and supplier. I'm sure for a more established company it would be much easier. The suppliers we work with today are proud of their products and are more than happy to share their production process with our public. In the end it is a win-win situation for everyone. We are building a positive reputation in a record amount of time; the customer gains clarity and the supplier gains notoriety.

You have said in an interview that Honest By is not an eco brand. What is Honest By then?

I believe that the term *eco fashion* marginalises the efforts that certain designers are making to create in a more life-friendly way. For me there is no such thing as eco fashion – there is only fashion and some of us produce it in a transparent, sustainable and responsible way, and others don't.

But what changed your mind? How did it happen?

Before I launched Honest By I had my own collection that I showed in Paris and I also worked for a German brand called Hugo Boss. I did not consider myself to be an irresponsible designer, I just didn't know better. I was unaware of the consequences of my choices and decisions. I was convinced that buying fabrics from renowned luxury suppliers was enough. I believed that expensive meant it was also sustainable. Which of course is not the case. Certified organic or other sustainable fabrics can be expensive sometimes, but expensive does not mean sustainable. After my sabbatical in India I became aware of all these things and it bothered me. I just had a change of heart. I believe changing my mind about certain things was the most important thing I did in my life. I remember I used to spend a lot of time trying to justify my lifestyle. I don't need to do that anymore. I'm proud of what I'm doing.

The fast fashion companies often argue that they don't know every step of their supply chain.

Neither do the luxury fashion brands. The high fashion industry is not more transparent or sustainable in any way than the high street part of the industry. That is a myth. It might have been true before, but it is not today. I can assure you there isn't one designer in Paris working for a heritage brand who knows who was working on that silk farm in India or China. Those dresses might cost a fortune because they are handmade in

"Open Source will change the whole fashion system."

Paris, but no one will be able to tell you who was working on those cotton fields or how the animals were treated when they were shaved for their wool. And that is just the beginning. The story behind the design needs to be as beautiful as the design itself; that is my mission with Honest By.

Some of the brands argued that transparency is not efficient. If you want to research all your suppliers, it costs much more money and the textiles will be much more expensive.

That is the kind of answer I would expect from brands that have things to hide. When how you work and where you produce is honest and publishable it is an advantage for everyone to do so. Everything is possible and it doesn't need to cost more for the client. That is simply not true. I have worked for large corporations and I've noticed that everything can be done if and when the customer asks for it. Customers need to understand that they are at the top of the fashion pyramid. They control everyone and everything. Whatever they ask for they shall receive. This industry, as any other industry, exists only to create financial gain. Its purpose is not to dress the world or make people look beautiful; its only goal is monetary growth. If we want brands to become responsible and transparent we need to learn to use the language of money. It is through our wallets that we can let our opinions be heard. Just having an opinion – while continuing to buy from these brands that are causing so much damage – will not change anything.

You are a kind of role model with your transparency aspects.

I do what I believe is important and urgent. Sometimes I do feel like I'm asking the blind to see and get frustrated and discouraged. But that kind of attitude is unproductive. Everyone is doing the best they can with the awareness they currently possess. Fortunately we are all evolving constantly.

In June 2015 you were the first high fashion brand to offer a downloadable 3D collection that could be printed out on any printer. You designed nine different 3D accessories in collaboration with the Spanish design collective Comme Des Machines. Why did you do that?

What I love about 3D printing is the fact that you could print it out yourself at home or through a 3D hub. Which is fun, democratic, ethical and sustainable. One doesn't have the damaging effects of transportation, which is fantastic for our environment. And there are also no labour issues anymore. Because you are the only manufacturer. And on top of that there is immediate and complete transparency. For young designers this can be a lifesaver as there are no minimum quantity orders required. There are so many advantages. I believe it has the potential to reshape the entire industry.

Do you really think that 3D design could be the solution to all these problems?

Maybe not everything, but – if we continue to develop this technology – it does have the potential to solve a lot of the problems we are currently facing. If in a few years we all print out our socks, underwear, T-shirts, etc., many things will change for the better. It's a new way of purchasing fashion as well. Eventually 3D printing could even become like Instagram or Facebook. Everyone would be able to offer their designs online and we could download and print out from one another. In the future everyone will be a designer.

"Be the change you want to see in the world."
Gandhi

Are you using sustainable materials for your 3D collection?

The filaments are biodegradable and recycled. Soon shredders will be launched that will be able to turn your unwanted prints into new filaments. You will be able to recycle at home. Some printers will also able to turn household trash into new filaments. How great would that be.

You have offered your 3D accessories collection for downloading as an open-source project. So you can use the files as is but also change them?

Yes, you can change the colour and so on. But if you want the design as we present it – which is usually what the customer wants – why would you?

Could customers take your design and put it into mass production?

Yes. It's like sharing MP3 files with music. That's why the music industry claims to be suffering right now. But none of that matters. If the public wants something it can not and should not be stopped.

We mean a lot of design is protected...

None of this will happen overnight. I'm sure all will be fine.

Do you think open-source 3D printing will change the future of fashion?

I hope so. But we are at the beginning of this. It's still a very new idea. At the moment it's limited as to what you can print out. There are no other brands offering designs that one can download and print at home or through a 3D hub. But I think it will and should evolve. Ready-to-wear could turn into ready-to-print. That would be nice.

In April 2013 there was the Rana Plaza tragedy when an eight-storey textile factory collapsed in Bangladesh. 1,134 people died; more than 2,300 people where injured. Do you think the customers are now more aware of how our clothes are made?

That story was published everywhere in the media and on the Internet. There are also documentaries about it, etc. But I'm not sure that Gandhi's famous quote "Be the change you want to see in the world" has completely sunk in yet. What comforts me is that there is a small group of people who are aware, and they are very influential. There definitely is a shift happening.

Everybody has to start within his or her own life…

Yes. People are starting to ask questions. And there is no better place to start than with yourself.

Do you live a sustainable lifestyle?

I do everything I know I can do. I became a vegan; I only wear certified organic or vintage clothing. All my furniture is vintage. The food I buy is local or all certified organic. My gas and electricity come from 100 per cent renewable energy. I ride my bike; I don't have a car. Everything one can do, I'm doing it. And when someone tells me I can do more, I do that too. It doesn't end. It makes me feel good and proud of myself.

Who inspired you to change your behaviour?

My youngest sister helped me a lot with this. She was already interested in vegan food, et cetera, before I was. What I've learned through making these choices and changes in my life is that now I find it easier to also love myself. When you are proud of yourself, it's much easier to love yourself. So being kind to others made it easier for me to also be kind to myself.

What's your vision for the future of fashion?

I'm hopeful. If we continue this conversation many things will change. We have all the solutions, we just need to start putting it all into practice.

What do you think are the biggest problems in the fashion industry right now?

The biggest problem is that the solutions exist – many solutions – but they are being ignored or delayed and the customer is allowing this to happen. But I'm sure this book will help to speed things up.

ROYAL BLUSH

JANA KELLER
BIRSFELDEN, SWITZERLAND

SALMON SKINS AND LEATHER

Jana Keller founded ROYAL BLUSH in 2006, shortly after completing her studies in Fashion Design at Esmod Berlin. She started with handbags made of leather tanned with vegetable dyes. In those days few people knew that leather was mostly tanned using chemicals that were harmful to the environment. Keller believed that people should be informed, discovered a market niche and went on to specialise in calf leather accessories that were tanned using tree bark and roots.

Her arm decorations, belts and rings are made of artistic knots held together with brass catches; part of the collection is plated with certified old gold. Where did she find the inspiration for these unusual forms? "I became fascinated by the knots during a canyoning tour in Austria and they became an obsession," says Keller. She subsequently had the idea of setting the knots in leather. Creating the perfect item of jewellery was not easy.

Because Jana Keller could not find a suitable sustainable trade fair for her exclusive accessories, in 2009 she founded the luxury fair Greenshowroom in Berlin together with Magdalena Schaffrin. The fair is held twice a year during Berlin Fashion Week. Keller ceased her involvement in 2014 on her own account and has since concentrated entirely on her own label.

In addition to calf leather, Keller now also uses organic salmon skin to make her bracelets, as well as using it to make espadrilles. The jute sole is covered with rubber so that these beach shoes can also be worn in the city. "My City Flats are an ecological variation on the new generation of comfortable espadrilles," explains Keller, "because we only use leather tanned using vegetable dyes for the upper material and the leather lining." So that her shoes are completely sustainable, Keller purchases the materials herself in order to retain the best possible control. The fish skins come from Irish organic salmon farms and are a side product of the food industry. The tanning is carried out in Germany and all the other processes are carried out by hand. The upper material and soles are stitched together and the inlays and rubber soles are glued by a Spanish family firm whose customers also include the French luxury brand Hermès. Only the adhesive for the soles is not a natural product; water-soluble adhesive is used so that the soles will last for more than one summer and carry on adorning the wearer, like Keller's rings, bracelets and belts.

www.royalblushbyjk.com

ROYAL BLUSH

Elevation,
Autumn/Winter 2014/15
(these pages)

Desert Bloom,
Spring/Summer 2015
(page 30)

STUDIO ELSIEN GRINGHUIS

ELSIEN GRINHUIS
ARNHEM, NETHERLANDS

FOLLOWING HER OWN RHYTHM

Elsien Gringhuis really wanted to achieve fame as a bass guitarist. At the age of twenty, however, she changed from music to fashion and studied Fashion Design at the ArtEZ Academy of Art and Design in Arnhem. After graduating in 2008 she founded her label, which quite simply bears her name. Her style is timeless, clean, chic and minimalistic, with innovative details – but elegant, luxurious and feminine at the same time. Quality is her top priority. That is also the reason why Elsien Gringhuis has followed her own rhythm since the Spring/Summer 2015 collection. She no longer creates a completely new collection every season but designs a basic collection which she calls Books. And this will be complemented each season by a number of styles, so-called Chapters. The individual items of clothing remain in the range for as long as the fabric continues to be available. "Why should we put a lot of energy in the form of time, money and high-quality materials into new collections and then throw out the ideas after just six months? It's totally crazy," says Gringhuis.

Fashion for her has a lot to do with style and comfort. "I love it when items of clothing cling to your body like a second skin so that you feel at ease in them." Gringhuis develops her clothes by draping the fabrics on a tailor's dummy. "That is when I have my best ideas," she says; "it is like making music: when I start, one idea gives rise to the next." She also finds inspiration in the flat Dutch countryside and its endless expanses, like her father, the painter Henk Gringhuis. Her designs reflect the colours of the sky – cream-coloured, pastel blue or an intense dark blue.

The designer places great value on the fact that her fashion is sustainable. She makes no compromises. In her designs she ensures that the patterns are innovative and insists that as little fabric as possible is trimmed and thrown away. Some of her designs therefore follow the zero-waste principle. The fabrics consist of high-quality sustainable materials, many of them with a certificate to prove it. The prints of the "Elementary Elegance" collection were created by the fabric designer Aliki van der Kruijs, who uses surplus dyes from the textile industry. The dyeing of the fabric is the most difficult aspect with regard to sustainability, observes Gringhuis. Together with van der Kruijs she has experimented with natural dyes, "but it was very complicated and therefore far too expensive for my collection," says Gringhuis. She very much hopes that the use of this process will be possible for her fashions in the near future. All the designs bearing her label are produced in the Netherlands; thus she supports Dutch craftsmen and saves transport costs. "Quality is not an act but rather a habit," is how Gringhuis summarises the essence of her brand.
www.elsiengringhuis.com

STUDIO ELSIEN GRINGHUIS

Spirit from the Sky,
Spring/Summer 2014
(these pages + page 36)

Spirit from the Sky,
Spring/Summer 2014

KOWTOW

GOSIA PIATEK
WELLINGTON, NEW ZEALAND

ECO-FAIR AND EASY-GOING

Anyone who establishes an ecologically fair fashion label in such a naive and successful manner must be a born entrepreneur. Gosia Piatek was twenty-seven and was working for the film director Peter Jackson when she started looking for the next challenge. She wanted to set up her own company, one that was ethical, sustainable and transparent. "Over a meal in a vegan café in Wellington a friend suggested to me that I should create a fair-trade organic cotton fashion label." No sooner said than done. One month later the design for the first T-shirts, which she had created with her friend and a pattern-maker, was ready. The NZ$5,000 (about €2,600) that she received from the state for her start-up were spent within two weeks. Fortunately Piatek's parents, who had emigrated to New Zealand in the mid-1980s with their two children, supported their ambitious daughter.

That was in 2007. Since then Piatek's label has been growing steadily. The idea behind Kowtow is minimalist and casual women's fashion made of fair-trade organic cotton at affordable prices: T-shirts and blouses, skirts and dresses, trousers, coats and jackets, and scarves. There are three collections per year.

"We work 100 per cent sustainably down to the smallest detail. And transparently, from the seed to the item of clothing," says Piatek. And so that they do not merely pay lip service to this ideal, they work directly with small farmers in India whose cotton is grown organically and has been awarded the Fair Trade seal. "The farmers plant lentils between the cotton plants in their fields; this makes the cotton grow better and provides them with food at the same time."

With this example of cotton we can see why the production chains in fashion have become so opaque. "The supply chain in fashion, in contrast to that for goods like coffee or bananas, is incredibly complex." That applies to the cultivation as well as the spinning, weaving, dyeing and even the stitching. So many countries are involved to produce just a single T-shirt. Kowtow sets store by long-term relationships with its suppliers. "We have worked from the very beginning with the same two factories. We have our jersey items stitched in Calcutta and the items made of woven cotton in Mumbai."

Now that Kowtow sells its collections throughout New Zealand as well as in Australia, Asia, the United States and Europe, Piatek is starting to think about other materials. Merino wool, perhaps. "But it must be just as transparent as our cotton," she insists.

www.kowtowclothing.com

KOWTOW

The Studio
(far left)

The Story We Tell
(left page, top right and
bottom right + this page)

47

MAXJENNY!

MAXJENNY FORSLUND
COPENHAGEN, DENMARK

DANISH AVANT-GARDE

Anyone who wears an outfit by Maxjenny! will find it impossible to hide. In her outdoor coats and dresses you are simply bound to be noticed: garish colours, wild patterns and innovative fabrics are the hallmark of the Danish label from Copenhagen. The exclamation mark behind the name says it all. Maxjenny Forslund, designer and founder of the label, does not like to soft-pedal. She studied Furniture Design and attracted a great deal of attention from the media during her first career. But she became commercially successful only in 2006, when she created her first fashion collection together with her mother, the fashion designer and artist Margaret Forslund: a brightly coloured collection of jackets made using a fabric manufactured from recycled PET bottles. "I was inspired by my mother's paintings," explains Maxjenny Forslund. Madonna wore items from the Summer 2006 collection in a music video. It was a fast and furious start for the self-taught fashion star, who always wears brightly coloured glasses and shoes with her own avant-garde designs.

Forslund partly designs her fashions – functional outdoor coats and jackets and dresses – using the zero-waste technique and ultralight, innovative fabrics made, for example, of recycled cassette tape, recycled polyester or Tencel. "I printed the patterns on fabric on a vast screen-printing table in my parents' house." From the very beginning she has designed all the fabric patterns herself. "I have discovered that no one except myself makes non-repetitive prints, so I expanded that and have made it my trademark."

Today the patterns are transferred to the fabric using digital or sublimation printing techniques and water-soluble dyes; silkscreen printing was too expensive in the long run. Forslund also works with artists from Sweden and the Netherlands. She produces her fashions in Denmark and Sweden as well as Estonia, Latvia and Lithuania.

Maxjenny Forslund's dream of having her own shop with a showroom and design studio attached was fulfilled in mid-2015 in the trendy Vesterbro district of Copenhagen. The next item on her wish list is a store in New York; Forslund has numerous fans in the Big Apple who love her brightly coloured, flashy fashion.

Forslund aims to grow organically. She has learned from the hype relating to her person and sets herself realistic goals. She could imagine cooperating with a sports brand, picturing her colours and patterns on sportswear or swimsuits. Umbrellas with her prints have already been manufactured. We can look forward to discovering which dream Maxjenny Forslund will realise next. maxjenny.com

VIVIENNE WESTWOOD

LONDON,
UK

FASHION WITH A MESSAGE

It's Milan Fashion Week and to the rhythms of hard electro beats male models hasten down the catwalk. "Politicians R Criminals" is emblazoned in huge letters across a screen. The theme of Vivienne Westwood's Men's Fashion collection for Spring/Summer 2016 says it all. A model throws badges bearing the slogan into the audience. Others are wearing the badges on their jacket lapels or on their T-shirts. Vivienne Westwood rose to fame in the 1970s as the "Queen of Punk." Her fashion has always been political. Thirty years on her message is that politics are responsible for climate change.

In addition to their punk attitude the models are flaunting the new handbag designs from the Africa collection. Vivienne created this line in 2010 in Kenya with a view towards promoting ethical fashion and sustainability in the workforce.

The items are produced by hand, from the weaving of the cotton fabric to the printing of the material using silk-screen printing to the decoration with embroidered beadwork and the production of the Vivienne Westwood logo, an orb with a planetary ring made of melted-down scrap metal.

In collaboration with the Ethical Fashion Initiative (EFI) of the International Trade Centre (ITC), a joint agency established by the United Nations and the World Bank, this project has been a massive success. The EFI Africa Bag Collection evolves each season and is presented in Westwood's main Gold Label collection as well as the Red Label and MAN runway shows, demonstrating its growing significance to the Westwood look.

"The Made in Africa Project is not a charity; it is a perfectly normal business designed to sustain a long-term cooperation," says Westwood. The facts speak for themselves: in the five years of joint work, the project has employed over 1,500 craftsmen and women from twenty-one different communities in Kenya. Three-quarters of them are women. They receive a job with wages that are higher than those normally paid locally, which means that they can feed their families and send their children to school. Moreover the participants are trained in craft skills which they can then pass on. Not only the families benefit; the entire society does.

Today Westwood's motto is "Quality rather than quantity." That applies not only to the Africa project with EFI but one which she makes a conscious decision to implement in all aspects of her brand. In an interview with the *Observer* she explained that she did not wish to expand her business any further. Instead, the company is considering the merging of all individual collections under one focused umbrella. As one of the few owner-run brands in the fashion industry, she can allow such a move.

The label Vivienne Westwood is owned by Westwood, her husband Andreas Kronthaler and Carlo D'Amario, who has been the managing director of the company since 1986. Most Westwood clothing is produced in the company's own production facility in Italy, a rare occurrence in the fashion industry.

Vivienne Westwood's famous quote "Buy less, choose well, make it last" appeals not only to consumers, but she also practises what she preaches within her own company. Her strong political commitment to the environment and global justice has now become the main focus at the heart of her creative work.

www.viviennewestwood.com

Vivienne Westwood was born in 1941 in Glossop, England. Before she opened her first shop Let It Rock with Malcolm McLaren in London's Chelsea district in 1971, she worked as a primary school teacher. The husband and wife duo sold T-shirts they had made themselves and fetish clothing which Westwood produced with her sewing machine at home. The shop at 430 King's Road became the cradle of London's punk scene and a meeting place for musicians, artists and eccentrics. Westwood still operates the shop to this day under the name World's End.

By the end of the seventies Vivienne Westwood was already considered a symbol of the British avant-garde. In 1981 she had their first catwalk show, "Pirates," in London, showing fashion with a romantic flair. It also marked Westwood's breakthrough as a designer. After separating from McLaren, Westwood met the Italian textile manager Carlo D'Amario, who has run her business since 1986 and is responsible to a large extent for the expansion of the Vivienne Westwood brand and the licences.

In 1993 Westwood married the fashion designer Andreas Kronthaler from Tyrol. Since then the pair have designed all the collections for her label together. Her fashion ethos hovers between punk and historicism and has its roots in traditional Savile Row tailoring.

Westwood's credo that all personal beliefs are also political remains one of her leitmotifs. Today the former fashion rebel and "Queen of Punk" observes that "the climate revolution is punk." Since the dawn of the new millennium she has supported numerous organisations and has raised awareness of environmental and human rights issues. Her commitment is also reflected in her fashion. Westwood, still a punk at heart, was awarded the DBE in 2006 by Queen Elizabeth.

With a design record spanning over forty years, Vivienne Westwood is now recognised as a global brand and Westwood herself as one of the most influential fashion designers, and activists, in the world today.

VIVIENNE WESTWOOD

EFI Africa Bag Collection,
Autumn/Winter 2015/16

Gold Label,
Spring/Summer 2015
(left page, left)

MAN,
Spring/Summer 2016
(left page, right)

Politicians R Criminals,
Spring/Summer 2016
(page 52)

MARIE-CLAIRE DAVEU
KERING GROUP

SUSTAINABLE BUSINESS IS SMART BUSINESS

Interview with Marie-Claire Daveu, Chief Sustainability Officer at Kering Group, one of the world's biggest luxury goods groups with brands like Stella McCartney, Bottega Veneta and Gucci. She talks about Kering's benefits from analysing the group's environmental footprint, why sustainable business is smart business and about Kering's sustainable visions for the future.

Madame Daveu, Kering was the first luxury group to put sustainability on the agenda and at the core of its business strategies. Your CEO and chairman François-Henri Pinault once said that "Sustainable business is smart business." What drives Kering to act in this way?

First of all, there is a strong leadership commitment to sustainability so that the company can go beyond compliance-driven programmes* and integrate sustainability into the business strategy itself. François-Henri Pinault is fully committed and believes that sustainability underpins a more successful and resilient business model. In our view, to continue being a successful business in the increasingly volatile world in which we live we need to react and adapt. And the key to doing so is in understanding the relationship between our business, the natural world and society. Our sustainability agenda helps us to understand our risks and see potential opportunities. In fact, the pursuit of sustainability is not only imperative in the face of our global challenges but also makes good business sense. There are inherent opportunities in becoming a sustainable business. We have already seen that sustainability stimulates innovation and provides new business development opportunities, which in turn create business growth.

What sort of innovations are they, for example?

We created the Kering Materials Innovation Lab (MIL) in northern Italy with a comprehensive library on the subject of sustainable materials and a team of technical experts in order to encourage innovation in raw materials, fabric processes and manufacturing and to make opportunities and new 'greener' solutions available to the brands. The MIL is an important service provider for our brands and supports them in their research into sustainable fibres and fabrics. The Kering Sustainability Department and the MIL also support collaborative projects that help to promote the use of sustainable fibres in our supply chain. We are currently working on silk, wool, cashmere and cotton.

Kering published its first Environmental Profit and Loss Account (EP&L) in 2015. What was it about?

The EP&L measures the environmental footprint resulting from our own business activities and those of our supply chains by looking at six indicators: greenhouse gas emissions, air pollution, water pollution, water consumption, waste disposal, and changes in ecosystem services associated with land use change. The consequences of these en-vironmental changes for people's well-being are then evaluated in monetary terms. We created the EP&L as a tool that provides us with information about the environmental challenges and opportunities in our business and across all our supply chains. Our consolidated group EP&L, which we published for the first time in 2015, has given us a better understanding of our environmental footprint and what is driving it. The EP&L analysis highlights where we can make more effective decisions when considering locations, materials, processes and technologies. It also drives innov-ation – not only as to how we source our raw materials but also as to how we can be more efficient across our supply chain. And also, in some cases, how we can replace conventional materials with innovative materials that have a lower environmental impact. Consequently, it increases our overall ability to reduce our environmental footprint and also to respond to changes in the supply chain, such as fluctuations in the

MARIE-CLAIRE DAVEU

After embarking on a career as a senior civil servant in the field of agriculture and the environment, Marie-Claire Daveu occupied the post of Technical Advisor to the cabinet of French prime minister Jean-Pierre Raffarin. From 2004 she was Chief of Staff to Serge Lepeltier, Minister of Ecology and Sustainable Development; in 2005 she became Senior Director of sustainable development at the Sanofi-Aventis Group. From 2007 to 2012 she was Chief of Staff to Nathalie Kosciusko-Morizet, first within the Ministry of the Environment, then in charge of forecasting and the digital economy, and lastly within the Ministry of Ecology, Sustainable Development, Transport and Energy. Since 2012 Daveu has been Chief Sustainability Officer and Head of International Institutional Affairs at the Kering Group.

quality and availability of raw materials. With the EP&L we are pioneering a new way of thinking that understands the value to companies of the natural capital on which we are dependant. We survey and evaluate this natural capital and speak openly about our supply chains and the environmental impact they have.

What were the biggest lessons you've learnt from the EP&L report?

Many of us were surprised to see that over 50 per cent of the environmental footprint depends on raw materials production – for example, where and how our cotton is grown. Consequently, we have turned our focus towards more effective decisions when considering sourcing locations, leveraging efficiency in processing and implementing innovative programmes around sustainable production of the key raw materials we use. An excellent example of this is our Python Conservation Partnership with the International Union for the Conservation of Nature (IUCN) and the International Trade Centre (ITC), with which we are contributing to the improved sustainability of the python trade and helping to facilitate industry-wide change.

Why do you measure the environmental impacts of the entire supply chain in addition to the activities of the Kering Group?

A large part of Kerning's environmental footprint falls within the supply chain. And the reason why we developed the

EP&L, and support corporate natural capital accounting through platforms such as the Natural Capital Coalition, is because of our belief that business needs to acknowledge and understand the impacts resulting from its entire business activities, even if they take place a long way from their immediate business operations or retail stores. Furthermore, if we really want to drive change and contribute in a positive way to the global challenges we all face, then we, and business as a whole, will need to be transparent about where the impacts really are. Only then can we all work together to help design solutions that will address our current and future environmental challenges.

EP&L is open source. Why is Kering freely sharing the methodology?

As I have mentioned, collaboration is a key element when it comes to sustainability. We can only solve problems like the depletion of natural resources if we analyse them more thoroughly. Therefore by open-sourcing our EP&L methodology and sharing our work we hope others in our industry and adjacent industries can work together to address our shared issues. We believe that changes will really only take place if we work across the entire industry and share our knowledge and ideas with each other. Thus, we open-sourced our EP&L methodology. We do something similar in many other areas, including the Python Conservation Partnership. Here, too, we publish the results and help proactively to inform others and drive change.

KERING GROUP

is one of the biggest luxury and lifestyle groups worldwide with brands like Gucci, Bottega Veneta, Saint Laurent, Alexander McQueen, Stella McCartney and Puma. For Kering, sustainability is more than a business strategy with a bunch of sustainability goals and innovative approaches. Kering developed the Environmental Profit and Loss Account (EP&L), a method to measure the risks and costs of the environmental footprint of all their business activities and those of their supply chain. In 2012 Puma, a Kering brand, released the world's very first EP&L. The Kering Group's first EP&L results were published in 2015 along with the open-source methodology. Kering operates a Materials Innovation Lab and develops new sustainable materials for all of its brands. They also run a partnership with the London College of Fashion's Centre for Sustainable Fashion with a series of educational talks given by Kering's executives.

What are the biggest challenges?

Typically companies do not know their environmental footprint beyond their own operations, but the greatest impact usually occurs in the supply chain. There is no real understanding of how a company's business activities depend on, and impact, natural resources and what the effects on these will be. This is a major hurdle to overcome. In order to create a sustainable supply chain one must not only focus on the key areas of environmental impact but also be efficient at the same time. This is, in fact, the reason why we are doing pioneering work here and why we developed the first-ever EP&L. We can use the results to pinpoint our environmental impact throughout the supply chain and to develop appropriate sustainable sourcing programmes and processing innovations to reduce and mitigate our footprint.

Could you give as an example?

Systems need to be in place to verify and certify sustainable sources of raw materials and to promote a reduced production of these materials, so that sustainable options can become more accessible and available. In the leather supply chain, for example. This is why collaboration must play an essential part. We need to learn to set and implement standards, and we must implement innovative solutions at all levels of the supply chain. In my view, if we act together in the sector as a whole we shall be able to accelerate these necessary changes and enhance the positive effects. But only if at the same time we collaborate with suppliers, with civil society, with academics and experts, and with governments.

Kering is an important test case for sustainability in action because of its size and the diversity of its brands. What are Kering's key visions for 2020?

We are currently working on our social and environmental targets that François-Henri Pinault publicly committed to attaining by 2016. These targets are based on our deep commitment to finding sustainable solutions that not only reduce our negative impact on the environment but also have a positive impact on people and society. They include raw material sourcing, water and energy efficiency, and ensuring the highest working standards. We have translated this sustainability framework into our overall strategy and throughout every area of the business, and across our brands. By 2020 we will have embedded sustainability even further in our business and supply chains.

By then we will have measured our final progress on this set of self-imposed targets and have a further action plan in place. I believe that through our endeavours, and those of our colleagues in the fashion industry, there will be far more understanding and awareness in society about sustainability, which will drive sustainable product choices and consumer awareness. I envision that across all industries companies will consistently measure and transparently report on their sustainability progress through tools like our EP&L and Natural Capital Accounting, and that sustainable companies will be rewarded for their efforts through the financial markets.

"A large part of Kering's environmental footprint falls within the supply chain"

* (p. 58) *Compliance-driven programmes: programmes for the adherence to laws, guidelines and corporate codes of conduct, and avoiding regulatory non-compliance.*

REFORMATION

YAEL AFLALO
LOS ANGELES, USA

FUSING SLOW AND FAST FASHION

Green climbing plants twine their way up the wall of the former bread factory, now the corporate headquarters of Reformation in the heart of Los Angeles. Yael Aflalo, the founder and CEO, started her label in 2009 and united design, production, photo studio, web team and distribution under one roof. "Our factory is the first sustainable textile factory in the United States," she states confidently. What is her recipe for success? She designs very feminine, casual women's fashion using fabric remnants, vintage clothing and sustainable materials like Tencel, and sells it at moderate prices. And she pays fair wages.

"I am convinced that fast fashion, sustainability and local production fit together wonderfully," says Aflalo. "Because we work with limited material we seldom produce more than forty items of clothing per model and colour." The label sources most of its materials from Los Angeles and the United States.

For ten years Aflalo ran the conventional label Ya-Ya. She became increasingly frustrated by the vast amounts of waste which the fashion industry produces. When she saw the environmental havoc wreaked by the textile industry during a business trip to China with her own eyes, she decided to change things.

Aflalo sold her label and founded Reformation: "In 2009 there were very few sustainable brands with trendy styles or well-fitting clothes that I would have wanted to wear myself." That was her market niche. To it she added a Zara-like concept, which Aflalo adapted for her company. Instead of two collections per year, Reformation produces a new collection every two weeks. Because she produces everything in her own factory, less than one month passes between the design and the finished item of clothing. So now she can satisfy the precise requirements of her customers. "You won't find winter coats in July in our collections, because I don't believe that the fashion calendar meets the real shopping habits of our customers."

You can tell that Reformation is very close to its customers from its special collections "Don't Call Me Cute" for women under 1.65 metres and "I'm Up Here" for women with a large bust from C to DD, both of which were created at the request of Reformation's customers. www.thereformation.com

DEEPMELLO

ANNE-CHRISTIN BANSLEBEN
BERNBERG, GERMANY

FASHION FROM RHUBARB LEATHER

Scientist Anne-Christin Bansleben spent four years researching a plant-based tannin for leather and found it in Germany's native rhubarb. In the rhubarb root, to be precise. "So that my research results didn't remain in a drawer somewhere, I founded Deepmello in 2010 together with some colleagues and had the rhubarb leather patented," explains Bansleben at the Greenshowroom in Berlin's exclusive Hotel Adlon, where she presents her collection of clothing, bags, shoes and accessories. "We have put so much passion into the development of the tannin, and that is why we have taken this unconventional path from research to the fashion business."

It is important for Bansleben that her rhubarb leather comes entirely from Germany. The label owns rhubarb fields near Magdeburg, the leather skins come from German organic cattle and even the tanning takes place in Germany. The gentle tanning process is extremely time-consuming but makes the rhubarb leather soft. It has a pleasant aroma, is breathable, skin-friendly and suitable for people suffering from allergies.

Deepmello dispenses entirely with chromium salts, which are damaging to the environment and the skin, during the tanning process. "Our rhubarb leather is biodegradable and can be returned to the natural cycle," explains Bansleben. The same is also true of the leather dyes.

Deepmello aims to convince by virtue of its designs. That is why the label works together with German designers like Esther Perbandt, Anne Gorke, Leandro Cano and Kaseee and develops the collections with them. Regardless of the designer the style remains classic, wearable, functional and very versatile: the business bags have separate, removable inner bags – a clutch for evening use. The covers for iPad or Kindle can be opened up like a book; interior compartments provide space for credit cards and pens. Dresses, skirts and blouses combine rhubarb leather with organic silk or organic cotton. And the sandals have a sole of fast-growing poplar wood, naturally also "Made in Germany."

www.deepmello.com

M.PATMOS

MARCIA PATMOS
NEW YORK, USA

SLOW FASHION

Reykjavik, Tangier, Beijing and Detroit: these are the stops of an architect on a business trip. Marcia Patmos designed a six-piece travel collection in merino wool for this imaginary woman, with which she could travel practically and yet luxuriously dressed through various climatic zones. It includes a reversible dress which can also be worn as a shirt and skirt, a belt which can be transformed into a passport and document bag, and a hat which becomes a sleeping mask when the rim is turned down. "Merino wool is very adaptable. It can be knit or woven, featherweight or very chunky. Light or heavy. Drapey or stiff. It can be cool or warm, packs well (wrinkle resistant), has natural Sun Protection Factor, is always soft against the skin… So in general, the perfect fibre for travel," is how Marcia Patmos explains her choice of fibre. Her fashions can be worn in various situations and in layers, depending on the occasion and the weather conditions, making them perfect for the modern woman. The collection with which Patmos won the 2015 International Woolmark Prize demonstrates the various skills of the New York designer with craftsmanship and high technology: hand-spun yarn made from merino fabric remnants; Japanese zero-waste patterns with which no fabric is trimmed away; and new inventions like elastic merino yarn, merino tulle and merino fleece. The yarns and fabrics are not dyed: the colour range extends from natural white to grey and brown to black. Parts of the collection derive from a partnership with knitters in Bolivia, with whom Patmos has been cooperating for some time. The weaving artist Isa Rodrigues created a woollen fabric which she herself artfully painted.

In 2011 Marcia Patmos founded her own label M.Patmos in New York, having previously been successful with the knitwear label Lutz & Patmos. "I believe in slow fashion, but I'm not an exclusively ecological label. Ninety-nine per cent of my collection is made of biodegradable natural fibres like merino, silk, cashmere, cotton, linen, alpaca and leather," says Patmos. She likes experimenting with knitting and weaving techniques, sometimes weaving cashmere with leather and placing emphasis on materials local to the factory. "In Peru, for example, you will find wonderful alpaca wool and artistic weaving and embroidery, and the same applies to cashmere from Mongolia. That is why we also produce our fashions there." Other items of clothing are "Made in the USA."

"Customers like products which are both sustainable and affordable. In reality, however, fair wages and the use of high-quality luxury materials lead to luxury prices, and that reduces the size of the clientele." But her concept between slow fashion, quality and wearable luxury seems to work. Demand is increasing and M.Patmos is expanding in the direction of becoming a lifestyle brand. mpatmos.com

AIAYU

MARIA HØGH HEILMANN
COPENHAGEN, DENMARK

THE SOUL OF BOLIVIA

In the Bolivian highlands some 3.5 million llamas live on the farms. They carry loads and supply milk and meat, but apart from the locals few people had expressed any interest in their wool. Until the Danish knitwear designer Maria Høgh Heilmann met a producer of alpaca and merino wool in La Paz, who was experimenting with the processing of llama wool as a sideline.

"For our first collection we were searching for some exceptionally valuable wool, and the producer in La Paz was the sole person who had machines for processing llama wool, but no customers for it yet." Since alpaca wool was big business in neighbouring Peru, Heilmann and her local Bolivian producer wondered whether something similar might not be feasible with the little-known Bolivian llama wool. There must be a market for artistically knitted clothing made of llama wool, which has a long tradition in Bolivia, as long as the designs and colours were adapted to suit European taste.

And so in 2005 Danish design and Bolivian knitting skills were combined to create Heilmann's knitwear label Aiayu, which in the language of the native population means "Soul." The style is typically Scandinavian: casual, simple and timeless lines and precious llama wool coupled with traditional Bolivian knitting patterns in subdued colours. Since then 80 per cent of the Aiayu collections are made of the finest llama wool, manufactured by a single wool producer. "We started with 500 pieces and we have grown together," explains Heilmann; the producer now also has other customers. Thanks to the financial support of the Danish and Dutch governments he has been able to expand his production capacity in La Paz, modernising the workplaces and equipping the factory in an environmentally friendly manner.

Tradition and modernity go hand in hand. "We encourage the older women in particular to teach their daughters the knitting patterns and techniques so that their traditional heritage does not die out. These ancient skills are so valuable and rare to find, which is what makes them unique."

Heilmann is in search of other materials "with soul, or a story," as she says, that would also meet her demands for high quality. A range of her collection is made of organic Indian cotton in India, and a small part is made of Nepali Yak and Cashmere products in Nepal. Heilmann is convinced that the best product is made at its origin, where the expertise to handle and process it is the greatest. The idea has been well received; in addition to the women's knitwear collection, for some time there has also been Aiayu Home with cushion covers and blankets for an attractive home ambience.

www.aiayu.com

AIAYU

Wear,
Spring/Summer 2016
(left page)

Wear,
Autumn/Winter 2015/16
(right page)

Home,
Autumn/Winter 2015/16
(page 76)

FOLKDAYS

LISA JASPERS
BERLIN, GERMANY

ETHNO-MODERN FASHION

With stylish clothing and accessories from Fair Trade, the Folkdays label shows that craftsmanship can look really cool. Cool, too, is the Kreuzberg office of Lisa Jaspers, one of the founders and managing directors of Folkdays: it is furnished in snow white. On the sofa lie scarves of cashmere, alpaca and silk in dove grey, dark red and with a grey and curry-coloured zigzag pattern. They were produced in the Kashmir Valley in India, or in Bolivia and Laos, where traditional weaving techniques are handed down from generation to generation.

How did Lisa Jaspers have the idea of selling these unique products in Germany? "In the fair fashion industry there are not many cool accessories which as a young person I would wear," says thirty-two-year-old Jaspers, who has worked as an advisor in the field of development aid.

On a trip to Guatemala Lisa Jaspers met the Norwegian textile designer Heidi Strom, who was directing the project Designers Without Borders with local weavers. They were both enthusiastic about the items which were being produced there by hand. Unique products of high quality. They believed that it would be possible to sell items like that in Germany and founded Folkdays in 2013. "We want people in developing countries to preserve their ancient crafts and earn money from them. But often they have no access to customers." Folkdays shares the profits with the factories, the craft firms and the individual artists: "Then they can buy new looms or sewing machines and grow too," comments Jaspers.

Twice a year Lisa Jaspers and Heidi Strom travel to developing countries and purchase clothing and accessories: unique, high-quality items with a story.

Their first shopping tour took them to South East Asia. "In Cambodia we visited tiny villages in Takeo Province, which has been the heart of the silk production region for centuries," explains Jaspers. The women there are still masters of the ancient technique of ikat weaving: silk threads are dyed using batik techniques and are then woven with great skill. The result is scarves with beautiful zigzag patterns. folkdays.de

Ikat weaving technique,
Spring/Summer 2015
(left page)

Spring/Summer 2015
(right page + page 82)

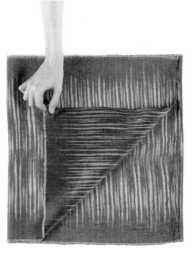

LEMLEM BY LIYA KEBEDE

LIYA KEBEDE
NEW YORK, USA

MADE IN AFRICA

Liya Kebede, supermodel, actress and World Health Organization (WHO) Goodwill Ambassador, had the idea of founding Lemlem during a visit to her home town of Addis Ababa. She was strolling through her favourite bazaar for handicrafts and admiring the traditional handwoven fabrics made of Ethiopian cotton when she realised that the artisanal skills involved were in danger of dying out. The reason was that fashion takes inspiration from the colourful fabrics and bright patterns of Africa, but high-quality clothing from Africa has become a rarity. Kebede, who lives in New York today, wanted to reverse this trend and make African fashion attractive again for the international market. Not through donations, but with the help of her own label Lemlem, which she founded in 2007. Lemlem means "blossom and thrive" in Amharic. The simple styles of the airy caftans, dresses, blouses and trousers for women, men and children with their subtle stripes in bright colours allow the precious handwoven fabrics to take pride of place.

"I founded Lemlem to help promote the art of weaving, to produce beautiful timeless pieces, while at the same time creating much-needed jobs in Africa," says Kebede. She is sure that by adopting this approach she will be able to help in a sustainable manner. Lemlem works with local workshops in Addis Ababa which spin, weave and stitch the Ethiopian cotton. With her label Kebede helps to provide over one hundred women and men with secure jobs with which they can earn their own money and support their families.

"Lemlem aims to be a role model for other brands. We want to show that tradition and modernity fit together and that it is possible to produce fashion of very high quality in Ethiopia." In this she is successful. Today Lemlem stands for fashion made with fine, hand-spun and handwoven Ethiopian cotton which is sold in luxury department stores like Barneys in New York and Harrods in London, or that can be purchased through luxury online shops like Net-a-Porter and MyTheresa.

In order to be able to keep up with the competition, Lemlem designs and produces four collections per year. The label is expanding. Already there are also handwoven scarves and ponchos made of merino wool and a home collection. Ethiopia, Kebede's native country, where she lived until she left school, is not however the only location. Kebede is also bringing her concept to other countries in Africa: "Kenya is our next stop," she says. In doing so she hopes to make fashion "Made in Africa" even more popular and to give people in her home continent a long-term perspective.
www.lemlem.com

JUNGLEFOLK

PAULINE MARIE TREIS
ZURICH, SWITZERLAND

MADE IN MEDELLIN

Junglefolk stands for urban, minimalist and sustainable women's fashion and accessories for the big-city jungle, combined with Colombian craftsmanship. The idea occurred to the creative Pauline Marie Treis from Switzerland, who has a degree in International Relations, during a journey through Colombia. While she was there she made the acquaintance of artisans who are still skilled in the traditional handicraft techniques. The idea of establishing her own label quickly took shape, and in 2013 Treis finally founded Junglefolk. Since then she has developed the designs; a pattern maker helps her to create the prototypes. The Junglefolk collections are produced in Colombia.

Treis obtains fine Pima cotton fabrics in organic quality as well as precious alpaca wool. The organic silk fabrics come from a cooperative for former coca producers in southern Colombia. All the fabrics Treis uses are environmentally friendly and fairly produced and are treated with only natural dyes. A craftsman produces the buttons using seeds, horn and coconut. Treis's fashions are manufactured in Medellin, the textile mecca of South America. A women's cooperative from the favelas sews the fashions as a cottage industry. "I have gradually built up the contacts with the women," says Treis. Most of the women originally came from rural areas and are still skilled in the traditional artisanal techniques such as macramé, knitting, weaving and embroidered crochet work. Most of them are mothers. For Junglefolk they work from home, not in the big sewing factories, and thus can be with their kids. And not only that. Treis works closely with the city administration of Medellín, which grants microcredits to the cooperative so that the women can purchase their own sewing machines, attend workshops and continue their education. "Some of the workshops we initiated together, for example on the subject of the manufacturing quality of clothes," she adds.

Since 2015 Treis has been concentrating on a single year-round collection, which she complements with summer or winter items according to the season. www.junglefolk.com

JUNGLEFOLK

Atemporal Days,
Autumn/Winter 2015/16
(left page)

Moon Safari,
Autumn/Winter 2014/15
(right page + page 92)

8 EDEN AVENUE

JESSICA GRUNER
MUNICH, GERMANY

CASHMERE — AN AFFAIR OF THE HEART

The ultra-soft, luxurious scarves by 8 Eden Avenue are made of the very finest cashmere to be found anywhere in the world. The wool comes from the same herd of cashmere goats in Mongolia that also supplies Hermès. Jessica Gruner, who founded the label in Munich in 2009, explains: "It was a huge stroke of luck. My Indian partner knew the owner of the herd and arranged with him for us to purchase some of his cashmere." For Gruner it was a matter close to her heart that the people who manufacture her products should work under fair conditions and be paid fairly as well.

Before deciding to set up her own business, Gruner had worked as a designer and product developer for brands like Cerruti, Adidas, Victoria Grantham, Diesel and Wrangler in Italy and Belgium. Now she creates the designs for her exclusive scarves and has them produced by Mukti Datta's cooperative Panchachuli Women Weavers in northern India. From the beginning Gruner's credo was based on top quality in both material and design. Not only is the finest cashmere used in the manufacturing process; the scarves are also woven by hand with great artistry and are then embroidered using traditional Ari silk embroidery. The craftswomen will work on a precious scarf like these for one to three months. Each step in the process is carried out by hand.

Since the dawn of the new millennium Datta's cooperative has specialised in the processing of cashmere. Today 800 women work there, in the mountain villages of the Himalayas; previously they used to labour in the fields of the highlands. Now they have long-term prospects for themselves and their families. By working for Datta they earn double the usual minimum wage in the region, and at the end of the year they are also paid a commission by 8 Eden Avenue. This enables the women to feed their families and send their children to school, and they also receive medical care.

Before the women begin to produce the precious scarves on their hand looms they are trained for two years in old weaving techniques. Gruner explains the journey from the wool to the finished 8 Eden Avenue scarf like this: "The raw cashmere from Mongolia is delivered to the cooperative in containers. There the women spin this exquisite wool by hand, then dye it, weave it and embroider it." You can feel that the scarves are made with love. Gruner's true recipe for success is that she combines quality with this labour of love. www.8edenavenue.com

MICHAEL BRAUNGART &
FRIEDERIKE VON WEDEL-PARLOW

"CRADLE TO CRADLE IS INNOVATION, QUALITY AND BEAUTY"

Michael Braungart and Friederike von Wedel-Parlow explain in a joint interview how Cradle to Cradle will change fashion and the textile industry.

Ms von Wedel-Parlow, Mr Braungart, please explain briefly what Cradle to Cradle is and what it means for fashion?

Michael Braungart: Cradle to Cradle is a design concept in which all products are designed in such a way that their materials can be made use of biologically or technologically after they have been used. There is no more waste. So instead of from cradle to grave it is from cradle to cradle. It is a matter of being useful, no longer being harmful – because there are just too many people in the world for the latter.

Friederike von Wedel-Parlow: Natural fibres like cotton, linen, wool, silk, cellulose and semi-synthetic fibres enter into the biological cycle. Artificial fibres, like polyester and polyamide, which are used for example to make jackets or outdoor clothing, enter into the technological cycle. Clothing is designed in such a way that it is either made of a single material or the materials can later be separated from each other so that a new product can be made.

Can I bury a cotton T-shirt in the garden and after a while it will decompose and become compost?

von Wedel-Parlow: In principle, yes, but that is not the idea of Cradle to Cradle. Cotton can be recycled mechanically so that you can make new products out of it. Or it can be downcycled to make insulation wool or furniture blankets and then composted later. It's not a question of the end product being compostable, but that fewer chemicals are used and that we know exactly which ones they were. Actually it's a profoundly social and cultural concept, because things are designed from the outset in such a way that they are healthy for everyone who has anything to do with them during the manufacturing process. Health means quality of life. That applies to people working in production, but also to everyone who wears clothing.

Frau von Wedel-Parlow, does the dress you are wearing comply with the Cradle to Cradle concept?

von Wedel-Parlow: It is an Armed Angels dress made of Tencel. The fabric does tend in this direction. The cycles of chemicals and water are very well under control in the manufacture of Tencel.

Braungart: Tencel is a cellulose fibre that complies with the Cradle to Cradle concept.

Why is the Cradle to Cradle principle so important for the textile industry?

Braungart: Because it is the most important industry worldwide. About fifteen times as many people work in the textile sector as in the automobile industry. But also because of its relevance for the environment. Half of all the waste water problems caused by industry result from textile production, and one third of all chemicals are used in the textile sector. It is no longer a matter of sustainability in the classic sense, but of innovation, of quality, of beauty. A product that becomes waste or that causes a skin rash is simply a bad product.

von Wedel-Parlow: Fashion has an immense power and can bring about change. Fashion is constant change, an expression of identity, of belonging or being excluded – and is thus both a seismograph of our time and a cultural motor. The first industrial revolution was started by weavers; today the fashion and textile industry could once more take on a pioneering role for industry.

What does that mean for the day-to-day life of a designer?

von Wedel-Parlow: Designers must have the self-assurance to demand and to employ quality. Designers can both spur industry on to innovations and also convey these new concepts to the customers. I think that at the moment we are on the brink of a new era because

FRIEDERIKE VON WEDEL-PARLOW

is a fashion designer. She studied under Vivienne Westwood at the University of the Arts in Berlin and also worked there as a lecturer. She was the co-founder of the label von Wedel & Tiedeken. In 2008 she designed her first ecological collection. In 2011 she founded the master's course in Sustainability in Fashion at Esmod Berlin Internationale Kunsthochschule für Mode, and has been its director since then.

MICHAEL BRAUNGART

is a chemist and process technician. He is the founder and director of the EPEA Internationale Umweltforschung GmbH in Hamburg, scientific director of the Hamburg Environmental Institute and the director of Braungart Consulting in Hamburg. Together with William McDonough he developed the Cradle to Cradle® design concept and is co-founder and director of McDonough Braungart Design Chemistry in Charlottesville, Virginia (USA).

access to materials, technologies and expertise is becoming easier.

In the Global Organic Textile Standard (GOTS) there are positive lists of the chemicals that are allowed. Do these lists exist for Cradle to Cradle too?

Braungart: Yes. It is important to define in a positive way what is in something. Because even such radical approaches as Greenpeace Detox produce lists of things which should not happen. The textile industry has signed the Greenpeace Detox agreement. It will then remove the 200 chemicals on the list from the production process and will use 200 others instead. It's like the story of the hare and the hedgehog. So we need to define the ingredients in a positive way, like a good recipe. That is important above all for industrial safety. Because the people in Asia mostly work without any sort of health protection measures and the waste water is generally released from the factories and into the rivers without being treated.

In fashion we still find very few Cradle to Cradle products. The philosophy and vision make sense. So why is the Cradle to Cradle concept not used more widely?

Braungart: Trigema's Cradle to Cradle products were launched onto the market in 2012, and those of Puma in 2013. Of course it takes quite a long time until they come back again.

103

With regard to Cradle to Cradle we need to look at the entire fashion system. It's a complex matter to get an overview of the entire supply chain. But Cradle to Cradle looks beyond the production and the use. We need to figure out a system to mark materials so that they can re-enter the cycle. And we need to communicate that to the customer.

In the Puma InCycle collection you get the impression that it was a one-off affair. Or am I mistaken?

Braungart: So far there are four Puma collections. The last one included 148 products right across the entire range. Puma makes available the list of ingredients in the InCycle collection for the public at large. Designers can have access to this list and can use it to create their own collections. And Puma also shows that new forms of communication are needed. If I say that these textiles are suitable for skin contact, what about the others? It is not a matter of green products but rather of quality.

von Wedel-Parlow: Today we need to talk at the same time about ecological and social quality. Quality, aesthetics and innovation are the three building blocks that the customer also understands. Because all the communication about less consumption or economising clearly passes the customer by, in cases of doubt we buy it anyway. But if we understand that it is a matter of quality and that something is lacking in quality, if it has been produced by child labour and is not skin-friendly, then I think people will be less inclined to fill their wardrobes with bargains like that.

If Cradle to Cradle is so complex, is it only a matter for big companies?

von Wedel-Parlow: Small labels are also inspired by Cradle to Cradle in their work and try to implement this design concept as accurately as they can. There are many new business concepts. Mud Jeans, for example, which with their leasing system for denim ensures that their products come back. Or labels that upcycle materials and take back old clothes in their shops, and also clothes libraries. I think that steps are important at all levels in order to close the cycle in the long term. The big companies will be necessary for the expensive development of new materials and recycling technologies.

Braungart: It's very important that people shouldn't try to be perfect. Although our institute developed the Cradle to Cradle system, I support copycats. If people say, "Based on Cradle to Cradle," "Cradle to Cradle in mind" or "Inspired by Cradle to Cradle," I'm satisfied. For example, if they simply include three, four, five Cradle to Cradle elements in each item of clothing. It could be the dyes, a zip, buttons. The main thing is that they aren't harmful. You can build up in a positive way on the non-harmfulness. You can say, "We need fifteen years, and the more you buy of it, the quicker I'll be." For young labels in particular it's a huge opportunity.

So Cradle to Cradle supporters need patience until the principle has become established?

Braungart: Yes. Six years ago there was no black which you could wear next to your skin without getting ill from it. It was crazy. We developed the first black for skin contact together with Triumph. Now I can understand that the people at Triumph cannot say that these bras are suitable for skin contact. But they reorganised their entire production. And that's great. And they did it without writing Cradle to Cradle on it. I believe that Cradle to Cradle will definitely prevail. Once you have understood that less bad is not good enough, then no one wants to continue with things that are not so bad. It took us eighteen years to acquire leather that

> *"Quality, aesthetics and innovation appeal to the customer more than foregoing consumption does."*

really can be returned perfectly to the biological cycle, and that is olive leather; the tannin is extracted from olive leaves. BMW uses it in its electric cars.

von Wedel-Parlow: The advantage is that the olive tannin functions in the same process cycles and at the same speed as conventional tanning. Other vegetable tannins are simply much slower and more complex. Olive leather can also be produced in large quantities in the long term. It could replace 40 per cent of the total tannin volume. Chrome leather is much cheaper, of course, but it is harmful to the environment.

Braungart: Olive leather also helps to stabilise bacteria as well as being very kind to the skin and highly suitable for shoes.

So in future will we all wear clothing and shoes that have been manufactured according to Cradle to Cradle principles – or what is your vision for the future?

Braungart: I think that by 2030 the entire fashion industry could change to follow Cradle to Cradle. Because Cradle to Cradle is being taught in many design schools. Because the principle values and celebrates people, and of course fashion is the ideal field for that. Instead of longevity I would prefer to see limited periods of use. Shoes might be labelled, for example, "Best before 2018." You could also take out fashion insurance and return the clothes after a defined period of use, three years for example. And then the various components could be rearranged in a different way. And I would suggest completely different production techniques. It is much more interesting to glue clothes together instead of stitching them. Adhesives can be made reversible; then you can use the materials again or reprocess them. That would be "Design for Reincarnation," and the next use would have been planned at the same time as the first one.

von Wedel-Parlow: Three years ago there was not much talk about Cradle to Cradle in the clothing sector. Today almost everyone knows about it, at least among the designers of sustainable fashion. About 30 to 40 per cent of my students complete their studies in this field. In my view it is only a matter of time until all Cradle to Cradle initiatives worldwide become interlinked and permit open access to materials, technology, insights and systems. I think we are on the threshold when that will all happen in the future.

MUD JEANS

BERT VAN SON
RHENEN, NETHERLANDS

JEANS FOR LEASING

After thirty years in the textile sector and after living and working in China and France, Bert van Son observes: "The textile industry is one of the most environmentally damaging there is. So today we should save resources – we owe that to our children." It takes an average of 8,000 litres of water to manufacture a pair of jeans. Moreover van Son, who comes from the Netherlands, dreams of a world without waste – although in Holland alone 135,000 tonnes of clothing are burned every year.

Because van Son wants to change that, he took over the bankrupt label Mud Jeans in 2012 and developed a new business concept: "Lease a Jeans." Van Son transferred the principle of the circular economy to fashion and has added to it a new consumer philosophy: to use the jeans instead of owning them. The jeans are made of certified cotton and are fairly produced. They are available in different cuts for men and women and they remain the property of Mud Jeans – the cotton is simply too valuable. "With my concept I want to create an incentive to buy and to show that sustainable fashion is affordable for everyone," says van Son.

If you lease a pair of Mud Jeans you pay €7.50 per month for one year, plus a deposit of €25. After that you can decide whether to return the jeans and decide on a new pair or whether to continue wearing them until you no longer care for them. "We repair, recycle or upcycle all materials and use them to create new products; that saves a great deal of water," van Son explains, "but also reduces CO_2 emissions tremendously."

The jeans that are returned are named after the first person who wore them and are sold as vintage. If they are too worn to be sold they are shredded, ground and spun into new cotton thread in Italy. After the zips and buttons have been removed, of course. When designing the products Mud Jeans makes sure that the recycling will be as easy as possible later on. Instead of leather patches they simply print a label onto the waistband in environmentally friendly colours.

New products are produced in Italy and Tunisia from the cotton thread made from the shredded jeans. However, because the recycling yarn has shorter fibres than new cotton, it has to be mixed with new thread. Mud Jeans uses it to produce pullovers and cardigans which are made of 85 per cent recycled cotton. Or they manufacture new jeans which consist of 25 per cent old jeans. This means that every pair of Mud Jeans is given a new lease of life, as a pullover, jacket or trousers. www.mudjeans.eu

PYUA

TIMO PERSCHKE
KIEL, GERMANY

FROM JACKET TO JACKET

A ski jacket becomes a ski jacket and becomes yet another ski jacket. That is a simple way of summarising the basic idea behind the ski and snowboard brand Pyua. The truth, of course, is a little more complex. Timo Perschke, the company's founder and managing director, worked in the market research and product development departments of a sporting goods company before setting up his own business. At the time he found recycled polyester from a Japanese supplier: "I was convinced by the material and incorporated it into our programme." Compared with the production of polyester from raw oil the energy consumption and CO_2 emissions are reduced to one-fifth, "and chemically there is no difference from virgin polyester," he says.

Because his large-scale customers were not as enthusiastic as he had hoped, in 2009 he founded Pyua with the aim of combining style, function and sustainability. His ski and snowboard clothing has the same performance values as traditional sports brands. "We test our outdoor clothing together with mountain guides in Lech am Arlberg and with ski and snowboard teachers in various places," says Perschke, "and so far no one has gotten cold or wet." He has his products tested in the same laboratories that Greenpeace uses for their Detox campaign. So far nothing has ever been found, says Perschke,

because his clothing is impregnated without any environmentally harmful fluorocarbons.

So that Pyua's ski and snowboard fashions are also recyclable, constant attention is paid during product development to sustainability. Jackets or trousers are either made entirely of polyester, from the outer fabric to the membrane to the lining material, or the clothing is developed in such a way that the different materials can be easily separated from each other during recycling.

Pyua acquires the raw materials for its clothing from old clothes collections via a textile recycling company, or from retailers who take back used Pyua clothing. "A jacket like this is simply thrown into the shredder," is how he explains the recycling. "Then we sort out what can be used again. Pure polyester is prepared for reuse and accessories like zips and buttons are transformed into building materials. Then a chemical recycling company extracts the colour pigments and later redyes the fabric." Pyua has to dispense with neon colours because they cannot be recycled. "The great thing about our process is that the polyester cycle can continue indefinitely," says Perschke. A ski jacket becomes a ski jacket and becomes yet another ski jacket.

www.pyua.de

LONDON,
UK

FASHION *W*ITH BRITISH HUMOUR

London, the East End. Aircraft from nearby City Airport drone across the district. In the workshop of Christopher Ræburn an atmosphere of concentrated calm prevails. There are two days to go to the fashion shows of the London Collections Men. On the cutter's table lie piles of jackets that look as if they are intended to fit Michelin men. An assistant checks the valves. Ræburn is a master of breathing a new lease of life into hot-air balloons, woollen army surplus blankets or maps printed on silk. He has tailored the jackets out of an inflatable life raft. "I bought it in an eBay auction for £50," he says. It was delivered in a capsule, "I pulled on the line and the life raft inflated itself. Inside was everything you need to survive on the ocean: food, water, a first aid kit," explains Ræburn enthusiastically in his little office. This find inspired him to create his Raft collection. He dismantled the life raft into its individual components and used them to create latex jackets, vests and rucksacks.

He does not have a formula for the creation of his collections. What unites his designs is the deconstruction of things to create something completely new: contemporary fashion. The material often comes from old Army stocks, which are available

in large quantities and at a favourable price. American *Vogue* described Ræburn's Inuit coat with the sentence "Remember the 4 R's: reduce, reuse, recycle, and Ræburn."

His first memory of fashion is of his father's army sleeping bag with sleeves and a hood: "At the age of seven I was completely fascinated by it. The sleeping bag was waterproof and you could spend the night in it wherever you wanted to. When you opened it you could slip into it and pull the lower part behind you like a snake." It was only after studying Fashion Design at the famous Royal College of Art in London and founding his own label in 2008 that he realised that this army sleeping bag summarised his idea of fashion: functional fashion, lasting high-quality materials and that hint of humour which is peculiarly his and which has become his trademark. His men's collection has now been expanded to include a line for women and accessories. Luxury department stores like Harrods in London, Colette in Paris and The Store in the Soho House in Berlin carry Christopher Ræburn.

In the very first year after launching his label the designer won the innovation prize of the Ethical Fashion Forum and

met Alex McIntosh of the Centre for Sustainable Fashion. The two became friends, Ræburn visited McIntosh's workshops, and McIntosh is now managing director of the label.

From the very beginning Raeburn backed several horses simultaneously by entering into collaborations with prestigious brands such as Nike, Barbour, Woolmark Company, Fred Perry and Moncler. Ræburn is the creative director of the Swiss Victorinox brand. "As a small firm we are like a laboratory; we try out new concepts and introduce our philosophy and our designs into large companies. It's really great," he says proudly. Thus both sides can learn and profit from each other.

The Christopher Ræburn brand is based on three pillars. Remade offers concept fashion with limited numbers of copies, like the inflatable jackets. British stands for designs using fabrics manufactured in the UK, including woollen fabrics. And then there is Lightweight with fabrics made of recycled polyester, jersey and cotton fabrics.

On the shelf in Ræburn's office there is an entire zoo of soft toy animals. "It all started with a dog which we stitched from the fabric remnants in the studio and then stuffed with remnants of wool." Each season a new animal is added: rabbit, squirrel, fox and so on. "The animals symbolise everything our company stands for: our own way of thinking and our sense of humour," says Ræburn and laughs. From the gift to the shops – which initially received an animal with the delivery of each collection – the company now has an entire collection of accessories. Incidentally, the mascot of the Raft collection around the life raft is a shark. www.christopherraeburn.co.uk

CHRISTOPHER RÆBURN

Raft/Immerse,
Autumn/Winter 2015/16
(this page)

Meridian/Ascent,
Spring/Summer 2015
(page117)

Deploy/Flight,
Spring/Summer 2013
(page 116)

Signal/Optics,
Autumn/Winter 2013/14
(page 114)

PATAGONIA

RICK RIDGEWAY
VENTURA, USA

RESPONSIBLE CONSUMPTION

Yvon Chouinard, the founder of Patagonia, laid the foundation stone for his company in 1957 with the pitons which he produced in his parents' yard. A keen mountaineer, he initially forged them for himself and his friends before the demand for climbing gear increased exponentially. In 1972 Chouinard began selling clothing, sleeping bags, woollen gloves and hats for mountaineers and called his company Patagonia. Today the company from Ventura, California sells clothing and equipment for every kind of outdoor sport, from climbing, surfing and skiing to snowboarding, fly fishing and trail running. Since the early 1970s the company has made the protection of nature and the environment a priority.

Today Patagonia campaigns for responsible consumption. In autumn 2011 the company placed a full-page advertisement in the *New York Times* on Black Friday (the day with the highest turnover in the US retail sector and the start of the Christmas shopping season) with the headline "Don't buy this jacket" above a photo of its best-selling item, a blue fleece jacket. "That was the first time that we challenged our customers and the public to think twice before buying a new jacket and to ask themselves if they really needed one," says Rick Ridgeway, vice president of environmental affairs at Patagonia. At the same time the advertisement described how much water and energy was consumed and CO_2 produced in the production of the jacket, in spite of the fact that it is made of 60 per cent recycled PET bottles and thus largely manufactured in an environmentally friendly way. The advertisement was deliberately placed by Patagonia on Black Friday and attracted the expected attention.

The company thus positioned itself as a pioneer in responsible consumption. Quite simply because it presented in a transparent manner the way in which the production of this jacket affected the environment.

According to Ridgeway, Patagonia's way of thinking and acting is motivated by the fact that industry now uses one and a half times more resources than the Earth will be able to stand in the long term, if it is to regenerate itself. "So it is a question of encouraging our customers to act with greater awareness in their consumption if we want to prevent economic collapse." Patagonia therefore manufactures products with a very long useful life, offers repair services and collects used Patagonia clothing which is sold again as second-hand clothing. Of course

DON'T BUY THIS JACKET

It's Black Friday, the day in the year retail turns from red to black and starts to make real money. But Black Friday, and the culture of consumption it reflects, puts the economy of natural systems that support all life firmly in the red. We're now using the resources of one-and-a-half planets on our one and only planet.

Because Patagonia wants to be in business for a good long time – and leave a world inhabitable for our kids – we want to do the opposite of every other business today. We ask you to buy less and to reflect before you spend a dime on this jacket or anything else.

Environmental bankruptcy, as with corporate bankruptcy, can happen very slowly, then all of a sudden. This is what we face unless we slow down, then reverse the damage. We're running short on fresh water, topsoil, fisheries, wetlands – all our planet's natural systems and resources that support business, and life, including our own.

The environmental cost of everything we make is astonishing. Consider the R2® Jacket shown, one

COMMON THREADS INITIATIVE

REDUCE
WE make useful gear that lasts a long time
YOU don't buy what you don't need

REPAIR
WE help you repair your Patagonia gear
YOU pledge to fix what's broken

REUSE
WE help find a home for Patagonia gear you no longer need
YOU sell or pass it on*

RECYCLE
WE will take back your Patagonia gear that is worn out
YOU pledge to keep your stuff out of the landfill and incinerator

REIMAGINE
TOGETHER we reimagine a world where we take only what nature can replace

of our best sellers. To make it required 135 liters of water, enough to meet the daily needs (three glasses a day) of 45 people. Its journey from its origin as 60% recycled polyester to our Reno warehouse generated nearly 20 pounds of carbon dioxide, 24 times the weight of the finished product. This jacket left behind, on its way to Reno, two-thirds its weight in waste.

And this is a 60% recycled polyester jacket, knit and sewn to a high standard; it is exceptionally durable, so you won't have to replace it as often. And when it comes to the end of its useful life we'll take it back to recycle into a product of equal value. But, as is true of all the things we can make and you can buy, this jacket comes with an environmental cost higher than its price.

There is much to be done and plenty for us all to do. Don't buy what you don't need. Think twice before you buy anything. Go to patagonia.com/CommonThreads or scan the QR code below. Take the Common Threads Initiative pledge, and join us in the fifth "R," to reimagine a world where we take only what nature can replace.

patagonia®
patagonia.com

*If you sell your used Patagonia product on eBay® and take the Common Threads Initiative pledge, we will co-list your product on patagonia.com for no additional charge. © 2011 Patagonia, Inc.

TAKE THE PLEDGE

this strategy encouraging conscious consumption is not purely altruistic; after all, Patagonia is a company which increased its popularity and sales through this strategy. "We do not claim to be perfect, but we believe in sustainable growth," says Ridgeway. What he finds most important is for Patagonia to put products on the market that do not cause unnecessary damage to the environment.

Ridgeway believes that the biggest challenge lies in explaining to people the consequences their actions have on our planet, and the impact on resources and society. Patagonia is doing very well with this strategy and will sell even more outdoor clothing and equipment in future.

www.patagonia.com

PATAGONIA

"Defined by the Line"
campaign, 2015
(this page)

"Don't Buy This Jacket"
ad, 2011
(left page)

"The New Localism"
campaign, 2015
(page 120)

FREITAG

DANIEL AND MARKUS FREITAG
ZURICH, SWITZERLAND

COMPOSTABLE CLOTHES

In a glass case on the first floor of the company's Zurich head-quarters lies a sort of puzzle consisting of scraps of cloth covered with soil crumbs and straw. They form the outline of a pair of trousers: the waistband and pockets are still clearly recognisable but the rest consists only of crumbs. It looks like something that archaeologists have dug up, but it is the latest business idea of the Swiss bag manufacturers Markus and Daniel Freitag: biologically degradable clothing made of linen, hemp and modal, a fibre produced from beechwood. The brothers dug up the remains of the trousers from the company's compost heap after four months and placed them on display beside the first designs of the F-abric collection: T-shirts, shirts and jeans for men and women, chinos and pinafore skirts in muted colours. Simple, robust basics for everyday wear.

But how did a bag manufacturer come up with the idea of producing clothing? "We were looking for sustainable work clothes for ourselves and our team and we simply couldn't find anything that met our requirements, which is similar to what happened with the bags," said Daniel Freitag. In 1993 the two of them stitched their first robust, rainproof messenger bag from a discarded lorry tarpaulin, a used car safety belt and an old bicycle tyre. The prototype was the beginning of a success story.

Markus Freitag explains what happened with their corporate philosophy: "We think and act in cycles; they permeate our entire lives. From the compost in the garden to our favourite form of transport, the bicycle. And sometimes we also revolve in circles ourselves." It took five years before F-abric was ready to be launched on the market. The manufacture of the fabric and the production of the clothes both take place within a radius of 2,500 kilometres around Zurich.

The Freitag brothers use the flax fibre linen and hemp from France, Belgium and Holland. They decided to dispense with cotton because its life-cycle assessment is less favourable, requiring large amounts of water during cultivation and long transport routes.

Not only the fabric but also the lining, the label and the woven strap will decompose completely after use. The new fabric withstands machine washing and does not fall apart in your wardrobe. In order to ensure that a pair of F-abric trousers will compost down, it takes the moisture and warmth of a compost heap and the help of its inhabitants – bacteria, fungi, insects and worms. All that remain are the buttons, which can be unscrewed and used for the next pair of trousers – an invention for which the Swiss brothers have a patent pending.
www.freitag.ch

FREITAG

F-abric
(these pages + page 124 +
pages 126 and 127)

Composted F-abric jeans
(right page, top)

Compostable woven strap,
shirt buttons and sewing
thread, reusable jeans
buttons (right page, center)

KNOWLEDGECOTTON APPAREL

MADS MØRUP
HERNING, DENMARK

FAMILY TIES

Three hipsters with a bicycle are standing in front of an iceberg holding up a sign bearing the slogan "Take Action!!" An info box within the picture challenges the viewer to "Think organic. Wear your brain." Further down on the website of the Danish label KnowledgeCotton Apparel you will find black-and-white photos of Jørgen Mørup, one of the founders of the company, and the company's first knitting machine.

KnowledgeCotton Apparel links tradition and modernity to create sober, casual men's fashion using sustainable materials. Founded in 2008 by Jørgen Mørup and his son Mads Mørup, today the company is one of the few successful sustainable men's labels on the market. That has a lot to do with the history of the Mørup family.

Jørgen Mørup had been operating a textile factory in Herning since 1969; the town was the centre of the Danish textile industry at the time. The firm grew and grew; soon it owned 150 knitting machines. Mørup produced clothing for well-known brands throughout Europe, including Marc O'Polo. And because Mørup was always interested in new trends, from the end of the 1980s onwards he also processed organic cotton in his factory.

"My father has a good nose for trends, just like me; but when it came to sustainable materials he was a bit too quick off the mark," says Mads Mørup, who previously worked as purchaser and product manager for various Danish labels and who had accompanied his father from his earliest youth on visits to factories as well as weaving and knitting firms.

In 2008 father and son decided to combine their wealth of experience and to found their own brand, KnowledgeCotton Apparel, with high-quality design and high-quality sustainable materials. They were both experts in the field. "At the beginning the entire collection was made of organic cotton; today 85 to 90 per cent of it is," says Mads Mørup. The rest of the collection is made of organic merino wool from sustainable animal farming, organic linen or polyester from recycled PET bottles. The clothing is produced in Portugal, Turkey, India, Taiwan and China.

It was only at the end of 2015 that the Mørups sold their last textile machine. Mørup Senior is gradually withdrawing from the day-to-day business but will remain in an advisory capacity. The combination of tradition and modernity to create a sustainable label was the right decision at the right time. Mads Mørup will continue to expand, perhaps in future into women's fashion.

knowledgecottonapparel.com

TONY TONNAER
AMSTERDAM, NETHERLANDS

EAST MEETS WEST

Tony Tonnaer named his label after his favourite tattoo, a Japanese koi. The koi is a symbol for wisdom and happiness and is one of the few fish that swim against the current. So Koi became K.O.I., the acronym for Kings of Indigo. The Amsterdam denim brand lives up to its name. Since 2013 the company has included in its garment range jeans and tops that have been dyed using natural indigo. This rediscovery has posed a number of problems. "The dye is extracted from the indigofera plant in India," explains Tony Tonnaer, one of the three founders and directors of the label. Entirely without chemicals. Jeans fabric made of organic cotton from Turkey is dyed using the dark blue or brown dye, and this is then used to produce K.O.I jeans in Tunisia. "Because it isn't easy to produce exactly the same shade every time if you use indigo, which is a natural dye, in the beginning the dye used for the jeans was only half indigo." But Tonnaer refused to give up. Since autumn 2015 K.O.I has been selling "Veggie Denim" jeans which are dyed using 100 per cent indigo.

Tonnaer is constantly searching for innovations for his label, which he founded in 2010 after leaving Kuyichi. "My inspiration came from the classic five-pocket jeans which Levi's invented at the end of the nineteenth century as work clothes for the gold-diggers in America," he says. Quality, sustainability and innovation are his guiding principles. Together with a love of detail inspired by Japan. "Japanese products are designed right down to the smallest detail – every stitch, every button, and even the packaging – and we at K.O.I. do things that way too." Instead of mass-produced products they manufacture quality clothing made with organic cotton, recycled jeans and Tencel. And so that the working conditions are right too, the label is a member of the Fair Wear Foundation. "You can wear our jeans for five to ten years," says Tonnaer. There is even a repair kit so that customers can mend their jeans themselves.

The special Red Light Denim collection was produced with used denim from Amsterdam. Together with the Dutch House of Denim Foundation and a charitable organisation that recovers used fabrics K.O.I. collected and recycled the denim and then processed it to make new denim fibres which they mixed with new organic cotton to manufacture jeans, denim jackets and a denim coat. The "journey" of each item of clothing from the container to the new product can be discovered on the website.

Because not enough recycled cotton and organic cotton is available on the market to adapt the entire denim production to more environmentally friendly fibres with a reduced carbon footprint, Tonnaer is looking, together with other labels and the Amsterdam-based Strawberry Earth Academy, for fibres which can be used to replace cotton. "We are testing flax and hemp, which are grown in Europe: they need little water, no chemicals and grow very quickly." The future of jeans may well lie in their past: the very first jeans were made of hemp.
www.kingsofindigo.com

LIVING BLUE

MISHAEL AZIZ AHMAD
RANGPUR, BANGLADESH

BLUE GOLD

The indigo plant which is the source of the precious blue dye has been cultivated for centuries in northern Bangladesh. At the same time the art of quilting with elaborate hand embroidery has also been practised for generations in the villages. Living Blue combines these two traditions; since 2008 the company has produced headscarves and scarves, kimonos and cushions of silk and cotton. All made by hand.

The idea of creating their own brand developed from a CARE Bangladesh aid project. "We were looking for a way for the farmers and especially for the women in the northern part of the country to earn a living with sources of income that supplement their traditional agriculture," says Mishael Aziz Ahmad, manager of Living Blue, who helped to develop the project from the start. The knowledge of the plants and the crafts was already there and only had to be revived. Indigo is still cultivated in Bangladesh, but the production of the blue dye from the plant had been neglected for 150 years. Under colonial rule the farmers were forced by the British to cultivate indigo, for which they had to give up their rice fields and other crops, resulting in poverty and hunger.

"We do things very differently today. Traditionally the farmers plant indigo between two food crops, as a buffer crop, because it enriches the soil with nitrogen as a natural fertilizer. The plant only requires natural rainwater, and no pesticides or fertilizers. We use the indigo leaves to produce our dye. Farmers earn through that, saving on fertilizer and on firewood, as they use the stems as fuel. We only harvest indigo during the summer monsoon season, when it is grown anyway and not as a substitute for other food crops."

Many of the people with whom Living Blue are associated are landless farmers. "We lease the peripheral and fallow lands from the local government and provide the farmers with indigo seeds, and then purchase the crop from them," says Ahmad. Some 2,000 farmers in northern Bangladesh alone profit from the scheme.

As a social company Living Blue directly employs over 1,000 craftsmen in six villages; most of them are women. They extract dye from the indigo leaves, known as True Bengal natural indigo, then dye the fabric, stitch and quilt – all by hand. "In addition to their own traditional techniques, we have expertise in *shibori*, an artistic and highly skilled Japanese resist stitching and dyeing technique, which we combine with hand-quilting in our products; and we even have a market in Japan," explains Ahmad proudly.

Thus entire villages in northern Bangladesh profit from the manufacture of Living Blue products. The people there have work and fair wages, a long-term perspective and – something completely new for the people in the region – medical care.
www.livingbluebd.com

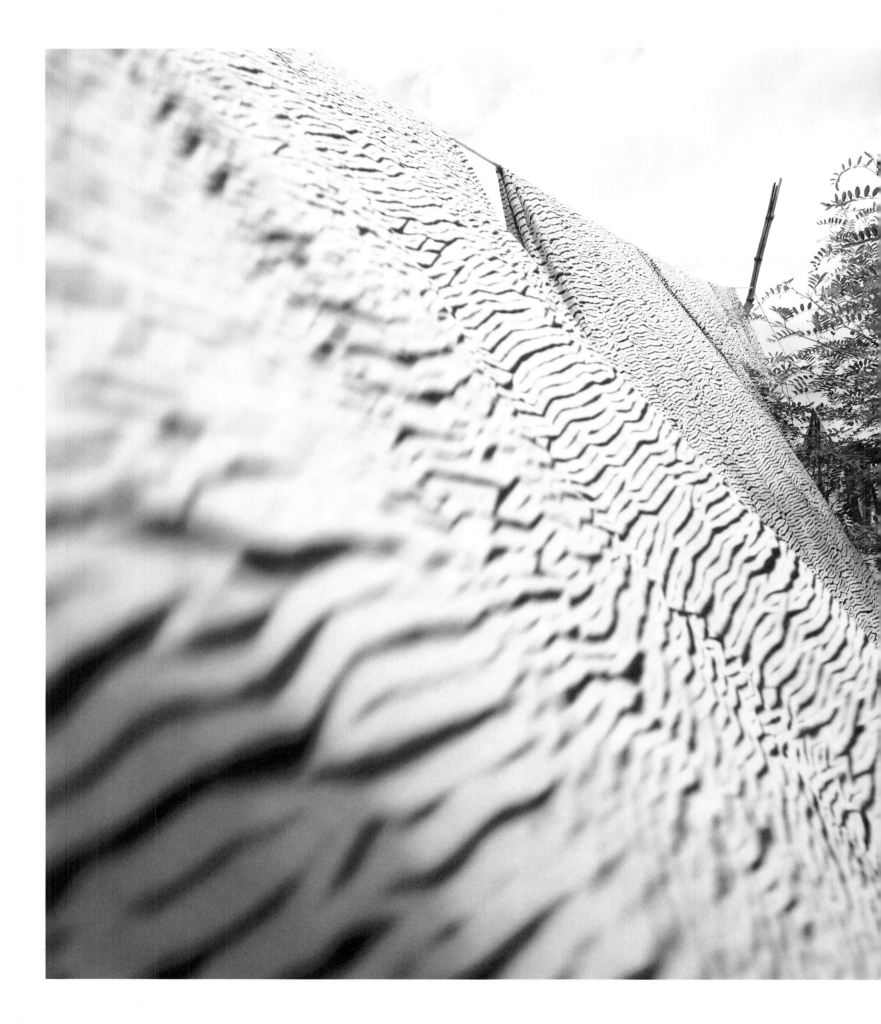

LIVING BLUE

Indigo Shibori Textile
(left page)

Indigo Shibori Quilt
(right page)

Indigo Shibori
Hand-quilted Coat
(page 138)

ORSOLA DE CASTRO
FASHION REVOLUTION

"THE CONSUMER CAN MAKE A DIFFERENCE"

Interview with Orsola de Castro, upcycling fashion designer and co-founder of the Fashion Revolution movement, about why we need a change in the fashion industry, the power of the consumer and her visions for the future of fashion.

Orsola de Castro, in late 2013 you started the Fashion Revolution movement together with Carry Somers, one of the pioneers of Fair Trade fashion. What has happened for you to demand a revolution of the current fashion system?

Over the past twenty years the fashion industry has been totally transformed, sped up dramatically, and that has resulted in very unsustainable and exploitative practices, for both people and planet. The fashion supply chain is broken. The problems are many and very complex, and persist partially because of the industry's lack of transparency. The tragic collapse of the Rana Plaza factory complex in Bangladesh on 24 April 2013 where 1,134 people where killed and many more were injured was a symptom of the broken links across the fashion and textile industry. A metaphorical call to arms, it has acted as a catalyst for those of us wanting to see change and demanding that the fashion industry take a leading role in achieving it.

What do you hope to achieve with Fashion Revolution?

We would like to see a future for the fashion industry where these problems are out in the open and ameliorated. We believe that if we start first by making the industry more transparent we'll be more equipped to understand the problems and then able to address the underlying causes. We believe in a fashion industry that values people, the environment, creativity and profit in equal measure. It is estimated that 80 billion items of clothing are delivered from factories annually worldwide. We aim to become the creative campaigning and reference platform for the fashion and textile industry's sustainable activities, promoting and supporting best practice throughout, bringing the message straight from the cotton farmer, the mill dyer, the seamstress, the designer, the stylist, the journalist, directly to the consumer; but we also want to operate at policy level and help to demand governmental changes. Fashion Revolution is needed because the brands, even the best of the brands that are working most proactively towards a living wage, cannot change the system alone.

With the Fashion Revolution Day you raise awareness and encourage the consumers to ask "Who made my clothes?," to wear their clothing inside out and to post a photo via social media or show it via flash mobs in different cities around the world. Could asking questions really make a difference?

Definitely. The best example was the huge success of the interactive photo booth in Berlin Alexanderplatz promoting a bargain, "T-Shirts only 2 Euros." By inserting the coin, a short video was played showing a textile factory where women and children work without a break, being paid only thirteen cents per hour for working under life-threatening conditions. At the end of the video an option displays "Buy or Donate." Most people who watched the video were in turn moved and shocked and decided to donate. The German team filmed everything, posted a video on YouTube and we had almost 7 million views online. In 2014 and 2015 we reached through our campaigns and actions 124 million people worldwide. Most of them via social media like Twitter, Facebook and Instagram. Fashion Revolution was also covered in hundreds of the leading national and international media outlets around the world. To answer your questions, we raised so much awareness in such a short time that I deeply believe the consumers – together with the brands and the politicians – can make a difference.

What's the problem with the current fashion system? Do we need a systematic change?

Yes. I think that there has to be a systematic change in the way that we review it. We are at that crossroads. I think that the new aspiration is the Internet. For so many years we have been sold a dream of aspirations only as consumers. We can't call a product "aspirational" or "democratic" unless it advances the people who make it as well. I think the people are really beginning to understand. Fashion Revolution, I guess, was one of the catalysts to underline that attitudes are changing. Before the Internet wearing a certain brand was your tribe. That was your sense of belonging, that was your sense of communicating. This is not needed any more: because of the huge success of Instagram and Face-

ORSOLA DE CASTRO

began upcycling in 1997 with her label, From Somewhere, the first to take luxury pre-consumer textile waste and remake it into new collections; collaborations include Robe di Kappa, Jigsaw, Speedo and Tesco. In 2006, together with her partner Filippo Ricci, she launched Esthetica, a hub for sustainable fashion at London Fashion Week (until 2014). In 2011 she founded Reclaim To Wear, an organisation bringing together academia, retailers and consumers to understand the issues behind textile waste, collaborating with, among others, Central Saint Martins College and Topshop. She is a regular keynote speaker at sustainable fashion events worldwide and associate lecturer at the University of the Arts London.

FASHION REVOLUTION

is a worldwide campaign to raise awareness of the negative impacts of the textile industry. Fashion Revolution Day takes place every year on the anniversary of the Rana Plaza factory collapse in Bangladesh in 2013, with different actions in almost eighty countries worldwide.

book where people communicate with each other, we can express our individualism. So I think the fashion industry will follow that "look." There is going to be a shift both aesthetically and in the way that we interpret aesthetics.

Do you live sustainably in your daily life?

I am a mother of four, so passing on sustainable principles is fundamental for me, in particular we recycle, upcycle, remake, repurpose. It's a family pastime. I drive as little as possible; I live on buses. I gave up my tumble dryer years ago and I am careful with my family's water consumption. So yes, I guess I do, as best I can.

What are your visions for the future of fashion?

I believe we will look back to move forward. We will rediscover values that speak of thinking smaller, we will embrace a return to a more localised industry, respect for smaller brands for their creativity and skills. We will demand complete traceability and transparency from the big brands. And we will avoid those that don't comply. Good will be cool and bad won't stand a chance. We will find a much-needed balance, where growth takes into consideration so many other factors other than money, and the words "aspirational" and "democratic" will be used to describe the entire value chain and not just the end product.

REET AUS

TALLINN,
ESTONIA

UPCYCLING EN MASSE

Beximco is one of the largest textile producers in Bangladesh. Some 200 million items of clothing are made in their factories every year for Calvin Klein, Tommy Hilfiger, H&M and Zara. Reet Aus, a fashion designer from Estonia who did her doctoral thesis on the subject of upcycling, analysed the production of Beximco. Her conclusion was that with the scraps of fabric thrown away there it would be possible to make 15 per cent more clothes. Initially neither the textile factory nor its clients knew the precise figures; nor were there any environmental analyses. Perhaps nobody really wanted to know all the details, because the environmental damage caused by the more than 5,000 textile factories in the country is vast. "Most of the fabric scraps are simply burned; but in Bangladesh there are no waste incineration plants that meet European standards, where exhaust fumes are filtered," says Reet Aus. "That is toxic waste, because the textiles are treated with large quantities of chemicals." Clean drinking water is a rarity nowadays; the energy reserves are no longer sufficient and Bangladesh has to purchase expensive energy from abroad. Reet Aus can easily lose her temper when talking about the subject: "There are solutions: the big brands and textile retailers must finally take responsibility. Upcycling is so easy; you can do it in-house and there is no need for large investments."

Upcycling hitherto covered fashion from old clothes or fabric remnants, produced as unique pieces or in small numbers. A good idea, but it was difficult to manufacture and thus expensive for the customer. Reet Aus also used old clothes for her first collections and worked with denim remnants from an Estonian jeans factory. "But it is very expensive if you only produce small quantities."

Reet Aus' research showed that upcycling fashion can also be mass-produced. Since her master's degree in Fashion Design in 2002 she has experimented with upcycling, and at Beximco she spent a year and a half studying the different types of fabric waste: cuttings, incorrectly produced fabrics and clothing, and overproduction. Together Aus and Beximco developed a unique system known as Upmade®. The upcycling takes place parallel to the production, so that even when the fabric is being trimmed upcycling models can be manufactured from the cloth scraps.

Their joint pièce de résistance was 23,000 upcycling T-shirts for a festival that were made from overproduction. "That was the very first time that upcycling was used in mass production," explained Reet Aus proudly. On the label attached to the T-shirts it states that during production savings of 70 per cent water, 90 per cent electricity and 70 per cent of CO_2 emissions were achieved.

Upmade® was approved as a certificate in late 2014. This means that others can also profit from it. "It's a win-win situation for both the factories and their clients. The textile brands and retailers can make larger numbers of items from the same amount of material and the scraps of fabric are fed straight back into production, which is of enormous benefit to the environment."

Since 2012 Reet Aus has been developing upcycling collections together with Beximco: T-shirts, blouses and shirts, dresses and trousers for men and women. She describes her fashion as "smart casual"; it is made from cotton denim, cotton jersey or Lyocell, a cellulose fibre produced from wood. The clothing is assembled from small squares, rectangles or diamond shapes. Each season there is a basic collection, which is then expanded with individual items.

www.reetaus.com

REET AUS

Autumn/Winter 2015/16
(left page)

Summer 2015
(right page + page 144)

HESSNATUR

MARC SOMMER AND MARINA CHAHBOUNE
BUTZBACH, GERMANY

GREEN FASHION PIONEER

The true pioneers of ecologically fair fashion are probably to be found in Germany. Because Heinz Hess was unable to find any clothing for babies that was free of chemicals after his son was born, he founded Hessnatur in 1976 and launched the first baby collection made from natural fibres on the market. Initially the company was a wholly mail-order retail firm for natural fashion. In the 1990s Hessnatur supported the cultivation of organic cotton in Egypt and helped to develop a processing chain for wool from the Rhön sheep in Hesse. In 2005 Hessnatur was the first German company to become a member of the Fair Wear Foundation, which campaigns for the rights of workers in the textile manufacturing industry.

Today, apart from its use of natural materials, the company supports sustainable production and social working conditions. It places more emphasis on design and is rejuvenating both the image and the product palette. Today the latter includes a complete range of products for women, men and children as well as a home collection. In addition to its mail order and online retailing Hessnatur now also operates its own shops at the company headquarters in Butzbach in Hesse, in Düsseldorf, Frankfurt, Hamburg and Munich.

"The sustainability aspect must also be reflected in the aesthetics and design," observes Marc Sommer, chairman of the management board. That is why the company hired Tanja Hellmuth of St. Emile as Creative Director in 2015 and works with young designers like Tim Labenda, who has been responsible for the men's collection since 2015. A project with master's students in Esmod Berlin, Sustain-ability in Fashion, resulted in upcycling collections of clothes and fabric remnants from past collections. Individual items from this project ultimately find their way into the sales of Hessnatur.

Marina Chahboune, one of the Esmod graduates, now works as senior project manager for sustainability at Hessnatur and developed together with Living Blue in Bangladesh a high-quality handwoven denim fabric. The fabric is dyed by hand with natural indigo, which is grown in the north of Bangladesh. "The idea for this project arose after the Rana Plaza factory collapsed in 2013, when the fashion industry partly withdrew from Bangladesh," explains Chahboune. Bangladesh has a long tradition with natural dyes and is one of the few countries where the indigo plant is still grown. "We wanted to establish ecologically and socially responsible production in the country and to make use of the raw materials, craft skills and local structures." Once again Hessnatur is a pioneer, but thinks long term and is building up the production in Bangladesh. "We will be the first to launch the 'Made in Bangladesh' denim fabric on the market, but later other textile manufacturers will also be able to purchase the fabric," says Chahboune.

In order to separate projects like this from the company's daily business, Hessnatur established the Hessnatur Stiftung in 2015. Through this foundation Hessnatur is consolidating its forty years of pioneering work in environmental protection, in textile ecology, in development cooperation and on social issues as its heads strengthened into the future. www.hessnatur.com

PEOPLE TREE

SAFIA MINNEY
LONDON, UK AND TOKYO, JAPAN

FAIR TRADE FASHION WITH BRITISH FLAIR

Clothing by People Tree, one of the classics among the eco-fair fashion labels, can be recognised by its feminine lines and cheerfully coloured prints recalling vintage clothing. You cannot tell just by looking at the collections that they all stem from Fair Trade. That is due to the approach of the British businesswoman Safia Minney. In 1991 she founded the development organisation Global Village in Tokyo when she discovered how little the Japanese knew about sustainable lifestyles. She visited weavers in Bangladesh and farmers' cooperatives in India and thought about how she could market their products. Before she went to Japan with her husband she had run her own agency for social marketing in London.

Minney remembers: "I brought designers and technicians together with the weavers and farmers. Together we started our first collection and sold it at eco fairs." In her catalogue she featured handwoven, naturally dyed handbags, clothing and clogs made by Bangladeshi women using fair-trade practices. The business grew and the development organisation became the Fair Trade fashion label People Tree. Global Village continues to exist in parallel. In 1999 Minney expanded into her home country, England.

Today the label develops 150 different items of clothing for men and women per season, mostly from organic cotton. The fabrics come from fair-trade enterprises in countries like India and Bangladesh and are manufactured according to the standards of the World Fair Trade Organization. "About a third of my collection is woven, knitted, printed and embroidered using traditional handicraft practices; the rest is machine manufactured. The handmade portion alone provides a livelihood for two-thirds of the people working for our organisation in rural areas."

Since 2006 People Tree has worked regularly with famous designers and celebrities. "We want to reach the fashionistas in this way and at the same time show designers what modern sustainable fashion from Fair Trade is." Emma Watson has already helped to develop three of her own collections; and for Spring/Summer 2016 the British designer Zandra Rhodes is creating a special collection called "Girl Power: Roses, Lipsticks and Bows."

Safia Minney knows how to advertise her causes beyond her fashion collections. In the 2015 documentary film *The True Cost* about the dark side of the fashion sector, People Tree was presented as a positive example of an eco-fair label. "We are a social business. Our main focus is always on the people and their environment," is how Minney summarises her vision. www.peopletree.co.uk

COCCCON, CREATIVITY CAN CARE

CHANDRA PRAKASH JHA
HAGEN, GERMANY

LETTING THE BUTTERFLIES LIVE

Looking at the patterns and details of Cocccon's scarves and clothes in turquoise, yellow, pink, red and orange you cannot help thinking of the bright saris of Indian women. That is no coincidence, because Chandra Prakash Jha, fashion designer and founder of Cocccon, comes from India himself. His home, the state of Jharkhand in northern India, is a centre for sericulture. It was there that Jha founded the project Creativity Can Care in 2012 for the manufacture of fairly produced organic silk, so-called Ahimsa silk (*ahimsa* means "do no harm" in Sanskrit). The project later gave rise to Cocccon.

Jha's aim was to create jobs in this economically depressed state, and to give the people who lived there a prospect for the future. "The silkworm breeders earn hardly anything from the sale of their cocoons and have no idea how valuable their work is. The middle men take most of the profits, and that is what I wanted to change," said Jha.

From the outset he found it important that after spinning their thread the silkworms in the cocoons should be kept alive and then mature into butterflies, instead of being killed in boiling water as is the case in traditional silk production. Now women slit open the cocoons by hand and wait until the silkworms hatch. Then they twist the silk threads by hand and wind them up again.

The Ahimsa silk threads are then spun, woven, dyed using natural dyes, printed by hand and stitched in Cocccon's workshops. Today the label produces in India GOTS-certified (Global Organic Textile Standard) organic silk entirely without pesticides, and employs a staff of two hundred.

Jha and his team are also working on vegan silk made with banana fibres; this is also produced in India. "It was a lengthy process; first we tested soy silk, but it lacked the sheen which is characteristic of silk. Moreover, soy bean farming frequently involves genetically manipulated plants, and I wanted to avoid that." It was only when they experimented with banana plants that Cocccon was able to obtain high-quality fibres which could be used to make vegan silk. So Cocccon now produces two collections, one of Ahimsa silk and one of banana silk, both of which are produced entirely in India. Jha also sells his fabrics to other designers in Germany and the United Kingdom.
www.cocccon.de

LANIUS

CLAUDIA LANIUS
COLOGNE, GERMANY

SELF-ASSURED BUSINESS FASHION

Claudia Lanius and her label are among the pioneers of ecologically produced Fair Trade fashion in Germany. Back in 1994 the trained seamstress and pattern-maker created and successfully sold a collection of jeans and dresses made of hemp; in those days she obtained her fabrics from Amsterdam. In 1999 she switched from casual and basic fashion made with hemp to women's fashions using natural fibres and founded her own label, Lanius. "It was from my very first customers, Hessnatur, that I learned that it is also possible to produce fashion ecologically," says Claudia Lanius; "I adapted their guidelines for my own label." Her company, like most of her suppliers, is certified with the Global Organic Textile Standard (GOTS), the strictest standard for ecological, socially responsible textile production.

Lanius's company philosophy is: "Show respect for people, animals and nature." She follows it with passion. The typical Lanius customer is a self-assured woman: "My patterns reflect the pulse of the times, and I give them a feminine twist." Even an oversized Lanius coat does not look androgynous but rather is available in soft eggshell colours.

Lanius likes to travel to the places where the fibres for her fashions are cultivated, so that she can check the quality on site. A journey to India to the BioRe project run by Remei AG from Switzerland impressed her greatly. Organic fair-trade cotton has been grown there since 1993. "As customers we give the farmers long-term purchase guarantees" – and that benefits both sides. A number is printed on the labels of her basic T-shirts. If you enter it on the BioRe website, you can see which organic farmer produced the cotton and who sewed it.

Lanius also likes developing fabrics for her label; her company, which has been expanding slowly but surely since the beginning, is big enough for her to do so. Lanius developed the fabric Ecowool® Sustainable Fashion by Claudia Lanius using merino wool from controlled organic animal farming. The fabric is available in two qualities, either as pure merino wool or blended with silk.

"I recently met a customer on the street, and she told me that she has had one of my articles of clothing for five years and that it was still as beautiful as ever. These are the things that make me really happy." www.lanius-koeln.de

UMASAN

ANJA AND SANDRA UMANN
BERLIN, GERMANY

FASHION FOR SKIN AND SOUL

A visit to the workshop of Anja and Sandra Umann, the founders of Umasan, in western Berlin. The identical twins have established their company offices in a plain Wilhelminian building in the Wilmersdorf district. Inside: parquet flooring and creative chaos, with clothes racks everywhere full of blouses, dresses, jackets and coats in black and white. Anja Umann, the elder of the two, quietly invites me to sit down at the expansive wooden table for our conversation. The twins founded their label for women's and men's fashion in 2010. "Back then, Umasan was the world's first luxury vegan label." The name of the label is a combination of "Uma" – which means 'Mother of Life' or 'Divine Mother' in Indian mythology – and "San" – respect for the uniqueness of the individual.

The name was not chosen by accident; the twins are vegans, practise yoga and find their inspiration in the Eastern philosophy of life. That is reflected in the Japanese accents that can be seen in the patterns.

Before they founded their own label, Anja Umann studied Fashion Design and worked for Yohji Yamamoto, Wolfgang Joop's Wunderkind label and Strenesse, while Sandra Umann was a photographer and art director for fashion magazines like *GQ*, *Vogue Business* and *Glamour* as well as running a makeup academy.

You will search in vain for wool, leather, fur or synthetic fibres at Umasan. Instead they use fabrics made from cellulose fibres produced from seaweed, milk, bamboo, beechwood and eucalyptus. Or organic cotton and soy silk. The garments are produced in Germany and Poland. "We use fabrics which are not only good for the environment but also good for us too, for our skin and for the organism," says Anja Umann. Her fashions focus on aesthetics and lightness rather than sacrifice.

Elegance and timelessness are two important words in the vocabulary of Umasan. The colours of their lines are white, grey and a great deal of black. Black summarises the Umasan style perfectly. "In our view, as a colour it unites the entire colour spectrum," says Anja Umann.

They design their collections around avant-garde basics which continue to develop from season to season with regard to cut, quality and colour nuance.

www.umasan-berlin.com

LILY COLE

"I'M ALL FOR
SLOW FASHION"

Interview with Lily Cole, model, actor and social business entrepreneur, about slow fashion, her social-giving network www.impossible.com, and how she met Nobel Peace Prize winner Muhammad Yunus.

You became well known through your work as a model in the traditional fashion industry, a big contrast to the belief in sustainability and social business. How do you balance these two very different worlds?

Working in the fashion industry exposed me to production chains in a way I wouldn't have been able to understand otherwise, and so I feel grateful for that opportunity to learn. Over time I have worked increasingly with brands that are trying to produce things in a more responsible way, and I am optimistic that we will see growth in that part of the fashion industry, perhaps one day to the point that it becomes normative.

You are the founder of the social business community impossible.com and co-founder of the ethical webshop not.impossible.com. What's the idea behind these two social businesses?

In 2014 I founded impossible.com as a platform for sharing skills and services to grow a stronger gift economy and community. One year later Kwame Ferreira and I founded Not Impossible (not.impossible.com) as a development of Impossible, as a platform for transparency in product manufacturing. The reason for Not Impossible was to encourage good business and try to provide a bigger audience and more economic viability for responsible manufacturing. And also to help consumers understand and navigate the complexity of supply chains so they can know better the impact they have with product choices.

Could you briefly explain the concept behind impossible.com?

Impossible is a community of people around the world who help each other through a pay-it-forward structure. The motivation was to grow a stronger sense of community and social cohesion through small acts of "kindness" and non-transactional exchange.

You mentioned transparency as a key focus on the website of not.impossible.com. How can transparency drive sustainability?

I think consumer choice largely drives business practice and political policy. It is hard for even the best-intentioned consumer to have a positive impact through their purchasing power if they don't have the information to decide which brands to trust and which production practices their money is supporting. So increased transparency is about giving consumers the tools and the power to make more informed choices, and this, we believe, will enable consumers to encourage more sustainable practices in production.

How do you select the products sold in the shop Not Impossible?

The initial products were developed by me or my partner, so we know the supply chains well and trust them. As we expand and invite in third parties we are working on a research and recommendation basis. We are working with several organisations in this space like Livia Firth's company Eco-Age to aggregate the research and auditing potential of multiple players and make the best appraisals we can of companies we think are trying to produce responsibly. Design also plays a role in deciding what to stock, as we think responsible products shouldn't compromise quality or aesthetics.

Your project is the first Yunus social business in the UK. So how did this cooperation with Muhammad Yunus come about?

I met Professor Muhammad Yunus in Davos in 2012, and then travelled with him to Bangladesh that summer for Social Business Day, to see the social businesses he had developed there. I was inspired by his concept of social business as a middle way between business and charity, and so we incorporated his tenets into our articles of association for Impossible.

What have been the greatest challenges in running a social business so far?

The Yunus Social Business model has been hard to find financial support for, as it is so new and so doesn't have an audience in the way philanthropy and normal business have. Also, it is very difficult to

LILY COLE

was born in 1987 and first stood in front of the camera as a model when she was fourteen years old. She has taken part in fashion shows by Chanel, DKNY, Jean Paul Gaultier, Versace, Alexander McQueen, John Galliano and Louis Vuitton and is regarded as the muse of Vivienne Westwood. She has appeared on the covers of Vogue, ELLE and other great fashion magazines and has worked with photographers including Annie Leibovitz, Bruce Weber, Irvin Penn, Karl Lagerfeld, Mario Testino, Patrick Demarchelier, Steven Meisel and Juergen Teller. She has also acted in several films. Lily Cole holds a master's degree in Art History from the University of Cambridge. In 2009 she became the co-founder of The North Circular, a sustainable knitwear and accessories label, and in 2014 she was also the co-founder of the social giving network impossible.com and of the online shop not.impossible.com. Lily Cole actively supports various charitable organisations in the spheres of environmental protection and animal welfare.

make a business work and even harder to make it work when you have lots of social and environmental restrictions! The products end up costing more to produce and you have to compete in a marketplace where people expect to buy things very cheaply with little understanding of what the true cost of making things should be if done the "right" way.

Why are you personally interested in the topic of sustainability?

Because I think the planet, nature, humans, are pretty cool and it would be nice to not blow it all up in the next few generations.

There's a quote from Vivienne Westwood: "Buy less, choose well and make it last." Should we all change our behaviour towards buying more sustainable clothing instead of buying fast fashion to save our planet?

I completely agree with Vivienne and have said a similar thing many times myself. Buying things you love, that were made with love, and that can last, be passed on and not end up in landfill is a much healthier way to approach consumerism. I'm all for slow fashion.

JOHANNA RIPLINGER

PARIS,
FRANCE

NATURE AS INSPIRATION

The model seems to float on air as she walks down the Green-showroom catwalk at Berlin Fashion Week in an ankle-length silk dress in delicate rust-brown, nude and sunny yellow. Johanna Riplinger's fashion delights viewers with its feminine style, which gently flatters those who wear it with flowing silhouettes and clearly defined lines. Nature is Johanna Riplinger's greatest source of inspiration. The German-American designer founded her label for luxury fashion using vegetable dyes in 2012 in Paris. "By the age of ten I had decided to become a designer," explains Riplinger, who then set about making her dream come true with great determination. "My first commission was to design a wedding dress for one of my teachers," she says enthusiastically. After studying at Esmod Munich she worked as a designer and buyer for various labels in Paris. When Riplinger met Rupa Trivedi from India whose Adiv project in Mumbai dyes and prints high-quality fabric using vegetable dyes she decided to set up her own business. "Respect for nature, people and animals was always important to me, and for that reason my entire collection is made of natural fibres," she says.

Parts of the collection are artistically dyed using the traditional Japanese *shibori* technique, thus giving rise to graphic patterns. Other items of clothing are printed with the petals of blossoms from temples in Mumbai. "Adiv employees collect up the dried blossoms, bring them to the workshop, separate the blossoms from the garlands, dry them and use them to print silk and cotton fabrics." The fabric is also dyed with vegetable dyes extracted from blossoms, leaves, stalks or coconuts. The dyed is fixed by means of alum stone, which is said to have the power to purify water. So neither the dyeing specialists nor the seamstresses come into contact with chemical substances. That is important to Riplinger: "In India vegetable dyes are often used, but they are mostly fixed by means of toxic chemicals and the end result is not much better than synthetic colours." She is particularly pleased by the fact that Adiv trains people to be dyeing specialists or seamstresses who previously would have had little chance of even finding a job.

Respect for nature and people will continue to be reflected in Riplinger's fashions, both in the designs and in the materials and production processes. www.johannariplinger.com

ALINASCHUERFELD

ALINA SCHÜRFELD
HAMBURG, GERMANY

ETHICS, AESTHETICS AND ELEGANCE

As an interior designer Alina Schürfeld has a well-developed sense for beauty and luxury. After studying design in London and Eindhoven she founded her shoe and handbag label AlinaSchuerfeld in 2009 because at the time there was no brand that met her high standards regarding design, ethics and craftsmanship. Shoes which lived up to both aesthetic and environmental criteria are still a niche product in the opinion of Alina Schürfeld.

He role models are the big international shoe designers. "My dream is for my brand to be mentioned in the same breath as Jimmy Choo, Christian Louboutin and Manolo Blahnik," is how she explains her vision.

Schürfeld's projects are designed to make her customers aware of values beyond design and to inspire. Because they tell a remarkable story of craftsmanship, quality and respect. Respect for man and nature. Since 2011 Schürfeld has sold her elegant shoes and handbags for men and women in her flagship store in Hamburg's elegant Eppendorf district.

Schürfeld creates the designs herself and has the models, lasts and heels manufactured according to her instructions in factories in Italy and Spain. Her favourite materials are salmon leather from certified organic salmon farms and Rhabarberleder® from Deepmello, which is tanned using vegetable tannins from German rhubarb.

"Actually I wanted to produce my shoes in Germany, but there are hardly any manufacturers of elegant women's shoes left here." Shoe production is very complex and it is essential to choose carefully the production firm that can implement the style, type and finish required. Initially it was not easy to find the right production partner. Today Schürfeld works mainly with small tanning firms which supply high-quality leather. "We share a common vision and grow together; that is both powerful and beautiful," says Schürfeld. For the designer beauty lies not only in elegant shoes and handbags but also in the masterful crafting of environmentally friendly materials.

www.alinaschuerfeld.com

ALINA SCHUERFELD

Electropolis,
Autumn/Winter 2014/15
(this page, top + page 178)

Heidrun's Sphere,
Spring/Summer 2016
(this page, bottom +
right page)

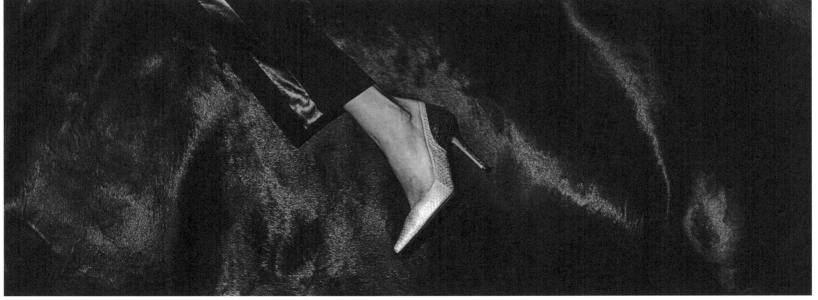

TITANIA INGLIS

NEW YORK,
USA

EXTRAVAGANCE FROM BROOKLYN

Titania Inglis wanted to preserve nature long before she became a fashion designer. That is no coincidence. She grew up in the liberal little college town of Ithaca in New York State, surrounded by waterfalls, lakes and forests. "For me it was always a matter of course that we should protect and respect nature," she says. Inglis started out as a journalist for daily newspapers, and for one year she blogged about sustainable fashion. She met many designers and the desire to try it herself gradually took seed.

Inglis learned the necessary skills at the Design Academy Eindhoven in the Netherlands and at the Fashion Institute of Technology (FIT) in New York. After internships and backstage jobs working for designers like Phillip Lim and Alexander Wang, Titania Inglis started her own business in 2009 with the label that bears her name: fashion that is beautiful without harming the environment. A small, luxurious collection for strong, independent women. Inglis's ambition is to dress free spirits like Björk or Tilda Swinton.

Her style is a mixture of rock 'n' roll and the beauty of the wilderness, raw and wild at the same time. The wearer should feel as if she were standing before a gigantic canyon, filled with awe as she gazes at the wonders of nature.

"I like wearing my clothes for a long time, frequently and on all occasions. My collections are therefore comfortable and versatile; you can wear them in layers, one garment on top of the other, sometimes elegant and sometimes playful." The dresses and skirts, jackets and coats, bags and accessories are made with her own favourite fabrics: fine Japanese organic cotton with its own texture and soft lambskin from Italy, tanned using vegetable tannins, which will only improve with time.

She paints certain dresses or blouses artfully and minimalistically or dyes the ends by means of the dip-dye technique. Inglis produces her collections with a family-run business in New York's Garment District. Her own workshop is in Brooklyn.

The biggest challenge for Inglis lies in the search for sustainable materials, which are much more difficult to come by than traditionally produced ones. And the second biggest challenge is the fact that many people still think that sustainable fashion is not fashion. "But I want people to discover my fashion through the design. And I want them then to feel comfortable wearing it because they don't need to worry that the garment was probably sewn by a child in Bangladesh."
www.titaniainglis.com

APPENDIX

SEALS FOR MATERIALS AND/OR LABOUR CONDITIONS

BLUESIGN: Awarded by Bluesign Technologies AG, Switzerland. Controls the chemicals and fabrics used at the beginning of the textile chain for resource-efficient and safe production for consumers and workers. Strict requirements with regard to water, air and soil pollution as well as waste materials and workplace safety. Generally used to certify artificial fibres found primarily in outdoor clothing and sportswear. **www.bluesign.com**

CRADLE TO CRADLE: The consulting firms EPEA International and MBCD developed the Cradle to Cradle design concept in 1995. For products that are environmentally safe, harmless to one's health and recyclable. **www.c2ccertified.org**

EU-ECOLABEL: Awarded by the European Commission for a range of products including footwear and clothing made of leather and textiles. Promotes the use of sustainable fibres and monitors the limited use of dangerous substances. **www.eu-ecolabel.de**

GOTS: Global Organic Textile Standard. Stands for high ecological standards in the cultivation of raw materials for textiles and textile footwear as well as socially responsible production. Certifies the entire textile supply chain beginning with the raw material. **www.global-standard.org**

OEKO-TEX®: The international Oeko-Tex Association is a union of sixteen prestigious textile research and testing institutes in Europe and Japan. Independent testing for harmful substances in fibres, yarns, fabrics and textiles. Certifies the following seals:

OEKO-TEX STANDARD 100: Testing for harmful substances to ensure compliance with the legally prescribed maximum values for harmful chemicals in the finished product.

MADE IN GREEN BY OEKO-TEX: Tests for harmful substances and takes into account social criteria. Using the product ID or a QR code, the textile chain is traceable provided that all production steps are certified.

STEP BY OEKO-TEX: A production certificate for textile firms to improve their environmental management and social criteria and to produce more efficiently. Certification requires compliance with legal standards and a Restricted Substance List (RSL).

www.oeko-tex.com

FAIRTRADE COTTON: Fairtrade International promotes long-term trade relationships in the cultivation of cotton and a transition to organic cotton; ban on genetically modified seeds. In the Fairtrade system workers are paid a premium for the development of social services, the use of which they decide upon independently and democratically. Refers exclusively to raw cotton, not the entire supply chain. **www.fairtrade.net/products/cotton.html**

FSC: Forest Stewardship Council. Seal for responsible forest and plantation management. Also applies to wood as a raw material for the manufacture of viscose, modal and Lyocell and to natural rubber as a raw material for shoe soles. **www.ic.fsc.org**

NORDIC ECOLABEL: Also known as the Nordic Swan; introduced in 1989 by the Nordic Council of Ministers. While the criteria are largely aligned with those of the EU Ecolabel standard, certain points are more strictly formulated. **www.nordic-ecolabel.org**

SA8000: Social Accountability International awards a certificate and checks compliance with the social standards for workplaces throughout the entire production chain of the textile industry. Collaboration with trade unions, corporations and non-governmental organisations to comply with the conventions of the International Labour Organization (ILO) and the UN Declaration of Human Rights and with national labour laws. **www.sa-intl.org**

TEXTILE EXCHANGE: Non-profit organisation founded to increase the cultivation of organic cotton. There is no focus on social criteria. Member firms include H&M, C&A, Puma, Nike et al. External certification for standards such as:

ORGANIC CONTENT STANDARD: Verifies all non-food products manufactured from 5 to 100 per cent organic material, such as organic cotton. The standard certifies that the information regarding the organic materials is correct.

RECYCLED CLAIM STANDARD: Verifies and inspects the origins of recycled material in the end product. The standard certifies that the information regarding the amount and type of recycled material in the end product is correct.

GLOBAL RECYCLED STANDARD: The standard certifies that the information regarding the amount and type of recycled material in the end product and interim products in the supply chain is correct, and also inspects social and ecological criteria as well as the responsible handling of chemicals. For products with at least 20 per cent recycled material.

RESPONSIBLE DOWN STANDARD: Down and feathers from ethical animal husbandry. **www.textileexchange.org**

UPMADE®: Certificate from Aus Design Llc. for the upcycling design method in the mass production of textiles, developed by Reet Aus. **www.upmade.org**

STANDARDS AND INITIATIVES OF THE TEXTILE SECTOR

BETTER COTTON INITIATIVE (BCI): The BCI was established in 2009 by brand companies including Adidas, Gap, H&M, and Ikea, among others, together with non-governmental organisations like WWF and PAN UK. The BCI aims to improve cotton production and the ecological, social and economic reality of farmers. In training sessions farmers learn how to increase their crop yields using proven techniques of cotton production from conventional cultivation with reduced pesticide use and an efficient use of water. Genetically modified seeds are allowed, as BCI cotton is not organic cotton. The BCI certifies the raw material, not the textiles made from it. **www.bettercotton.org**

BIORE®: Organic cotton textiles from the Swiss company Remei AG. The standard regulates the processing of the organic cotton from its own cultivation projects in India and Tanzania. Complete transparency regarding production via a Track & Trace system. The BioRe Foundation promotes the organic farming of cotton and campaigns against genetically modified seed as well as supporting social projects relating to health, nutrition and education. **www.biore.ch**

BUSINESS SOCIAL COMPLIANCE INITIATIVE (BSCI): Initiative to improve labour conditions in factories and farms through the BSCI Code of Conduct for retailers, importers and brands. The code is based on the conventions of the International Labour Organization (ILO) and local laws. BSCI does not perform audits itself and does not issue certificates, but it provides support to companies for their compliance with the Code of Conduct. **www.bsci-intl.org**

COTTON MADE IN AFRICA (CMIA): An initiative of the Aid by Trade Foundation, founded by the Otto Group, and supported by textile companies and organisations like the WWF and GIZ. Helping small cotton farmers and their families in Sub-Saharan Africa to help themselves. Efficient use of pesticides and artificial fertilizers as well as water management. Genetically modified seeds allowed; not organic cotton. **www.cotton-made-in-africa.com**

ETHICAL TRADING INITIATIVE: Association of companies, trade unions and non-governmental organisations to improve workers' rights in the textile sector; based on guidelines of the International Labour Organisation (ILO). The ETI forms strategic alliances between local organisations and international firms, carries out lobbying work, informs workers about their rights and supports them in forming trade unions and taking other measures to improve labour conditions. **www.ethicaltrade.org**

ORGANISATIONS WORKING ON SOCIAL JUSTICE ISSUES

ASIA FLOORWAGE ALLIANCE: Global alliance of trade unions and worker and human rights organisations supporting fair wages for garment workers in Asia. **asia.floorwage.org**

BANGLADESH ACCORD ON FIRE & SAFETY: Agreement between textile retailers, brands and trade unions specifically for the inspection of building safety in textile factories in Bangladesh. Negotiated after the collapse of the Rana Plaza textile factory in Dhaka in 2013.
www.bangladeshaccord.org

CLEAN CLOTHES CAMPAIGN: International initiative supported by local non-governmental organisations. Campaigns to improve labour conditions and supports workers and their rights in the global textile and fashion industry.
www.cleanclothes.org

FAIR WEAR FOUNDATION: Independent non-profit organisation. Collaborates with firms and textile factories to improve labour conditions for garment workers and to pursue higher standards in the manufacture of textiles, including monitoring by local independent inspectors.
www.fairwear.org

FAIR LABOR ASSOCIATION [FLA]: The Fair Labor Association is a collaborative effort of companies, colleges and universities and non-governmental organisations to improve labour conditions along the entire production chain of the textile industry, which includes internal and external monitoring. **www.fairlabor.org**

INTERNATIONAL LABOUR ORGANIZATION (ILO): Specialised agency of the United Nations where governments and employers' and workers' organizations cooperate to set labour standards guaranteeing freedom, equality, safety and respect for human rights. Initiatives include regulating work days and weeks, prohibitions on forced and child labour, regulating work by young people and monitoring the right to freedom of assembly.
www.ilo.org

WORLD FAIR TRADE ORGANIZATION (WFTO):
Global network of fair-trade organisations, companies and individual members. Membership and use of the logo is possible if it can be proven that the ten fair-trade criteria are complied with.
www.wfto.com

ORGANISATIONS WORKING ON ENVIRONMENTAL ISSUES

GREENPEACE DETOX: Regular testing of various textiles for environmentally harmful substances. Participating textile companies are obliged to exclude dangerous chemicals in textiles by 2020, including regular testing for harmful substances.
www.greenpeace.org/international/en/campaigns/detox

HOUSE OF DENIM: Charitable organisation for the promotion of innovation and sustainability in the denim industry in Amsterdam, Netherlands. **www.houseofdenim.org**

MADE-BY: This not-for-profit organisation supports companies in improving the ecological and social conditions in their supply chain. Made-By develops tools and evaluation criteria and makes them available to the public. Companies that cooperate with the organisation can demonstrate their improvements publicly and communicate these verified actions via a tracking system. **www.made-by.org**

UNIVERSITIES AND RESEARCH INSTITUTES

ARTEZ INSTITUTE OF THE ARTS:
Bachelor's and master's study courses in Fashion Design and Fashion Strategy as well as Design, Art, Music and Architecture in Arnhem, Netherlands. **www.artez.nl**

ESMOD BERLIN:
International University of Art for Fashion, private fashion university with a master's course in Sustainability in Fashion in Berlin, Germany. **www.esmod.de**

CENTRAL SAINT MARTINS:
Famous bachelor's and master's study courses in Fashion Design and Fashion Communication at the University of the Arts London, UK. **www.arts.ac.uk/csm**

CENTRE FOR SUSTAINABLE FASHION: Research centre of the University of the Arts London and the London College of Fashion, UK. **www.sustainable-fashion.com**

DESIGN ACADEMY EINDHOVEN:
Interdisciplinary Design study course with bachelor's and master's degrees. Main focus on conceptual and innovative design in Eindhoven, Netherlands. **www.designacademy.nl**

FASHION INSTITUTE OF TECHNOLOGY (FIT):
College for design, fashion, art, communication and economics in New York, USA. **www.fitnyc.edu**

GREENLAB:
Research lab for innovative concepts, sustainable and environmentally friendly products and services at the Kunsthochschule Berlin Weissensee, Germany. **www.kh-berlin.de/hochschule/forschung/greenlab.html**

HOCHSCHULE NIEDERRHEIN ETHNA:
Research lab in the field of Corporate Social Responsibility, with study possibilities and research projects. Textiles engineers are also trained at the university. **www.hs-niederrhein.de/forschung/ethna**

THE NEW SCHOOL, PARSONS SCHOOL OF DESIGN:
Renowned university for fashion design with famous alumni including Donna Karan, Marc Jacobs, Tom Ford and Proenza Schouler. Main focus lies on design, innovation, craftsmanship, marketing and environment aspects. **www.newschool.edu/parsons**

STRAWBERRY EARTH ACADEMY:
International academy for fashion and design professionals for the promotion of a fair and green economy in Amsterdam, Netherlands. **www.strawberryearth.com**

TED'S TEN:
Set of ten sustainable design strategies for textile and fashion designers, developed by the Textile Environmental Design (TED) research group, now part of the University of the Arts London's Textile Futures Research Centre, UK. **www.tedresearch.net**

SELECTED BLOGS

BOF, The Business of Fashion: www.businessoffashion.com

Coco Eco Magazine: cocoecomag.com

Eco Fashion Talk: www.ecofashiontalk.com

Ecotextile News: www.ecotextile.com

Ecouterre: www.ecouterre.com

Huff Post Ecofabulous: www.huffingtonpost.com/news/ecofabulous

Magnifeco: magnifeco.com

The Guardian, Sustainable Fashion: www.theguardian.com/sustainable-business/sustainable-fashion-blog

Dariadaria: dariadaria.com (German + English)

Get Changed: www.getchanged.net (German + English)

The Upcycling Fashion Store: upcycling-fashion.com (German + English)

Ecoenvie: ecoenvie.de (German)

Grüne Mode: www.gruenemode.de (German)

Grün ist das neue Schwarz: www.gruenistdasneueschwarz.de (German)

modeaffaire: www.modeaffaire.de (German)

Re:blog: www.otto.de/reblog (German)

ACKNOWLEDGEMENTS

A book is a highly complex project, from the development of the concept to the search for a publisher and the actual execution. We were accompanied during this process by a number of people whom we would like to thank for their support. Without it this book would never have reached publication. First of all we would like to thank Julie Kiefer, our editor at Prestel Verlag, for the enthusiastic discussions about the content and form of the book. We also thank all our interview partners for the interesting conversations and for providing the photos.

We are grateful to Alex Vogt, who went over the appendix with an expert eye, Djahle Krebs and Gerrit Winterstein for the inspiring discussions about the cover and title, and Kathrin Harms for the photos of the authors. And finally we would also like to thank Martin Jönsson and the Raumstation, who provided us with support during the busiest times.

SOURCES

ISABELL DE HILLERIN:
Interview with Isabell de Hillerin, 14.08.15, Berlin

HELLEN VAN REES:
Interview with Hellen van Rees, 10.07.14, Berlin

HONEST BY + INTERVIEW BRUNO PIETERS:
Interview with Bruno Pieters, 15.06.15, Antwerp
Zsuzsanna Toth, "Bruno Pieters, Fashion Designer, Penthouse, Antwerp," *Freunde von Freunden*, 13.08.14, www.freundevonfreunden.com/interviews/bruno-pieters/
Rana Toofanian, "Bruno Pieters – Honesty is the best policy," *Ever Manifesto*, 07.05.14, www.evermanifesto.com/issues/issue-03/honesty-is-the-best-policy
Annabel Fernandes, "Bruno Pieters – Honest By," *purple magazine*, no. 21, S/S 2014, www.purple.fr/article/bruno-pieters/

ROYAL BLUSH:
Interview with Jana Keller, 10.07.14, Berlin + telephone interview, 10.03.15

STUDIO ELSIEN GRINGHUIS:
Skype interview with Elsien Gringhuis, 12.07.15

KOWTOW:
Skype interview with Gosia Piatek, 23.07.15

MAXJENNY!:
Skype interview with Maxjenny Forslund, 22.04.15

VIVIENNE WESTWOOD:
Interview with Brigitte Stepputtis, 05.06.15, London
Vivienne Westwood + Ian Kelly, *Vivienne Westwood*, London: Picador, 2014
Vanessa Thorpe, "Vivienne Westwood: Climate change, not fashion, is now my priority," *The Guardian*, 08.02.14, www.theguardian.com/lifeandstyle/2014/feb/08/vivienne-westwood-arctic-campaign
"Vivienne Westwood: Everyone buys too many clothes," *The Telegraph*, 08.09.13, http://fashion.telegraph.co.uk/news-features/TMG10312077/Vivienne-Westwood-Everyone-buys-too-many-clothes.html

KERING GROUP:
Email interview with Marie-Claire Daveu, 30.09.15
Harriet Quick, "Planet fashion: On how consumers demand ethics to match their aesthetics," *Wallpaper*, 28.07.15, www.wallpaper.com/fashion/planet-fashion-on-how-consumers-demand-ethics-to-match-their-aesthetics/9333#124284

REFORMATION:
Email interview with Yael Aflalo, 16.07.15

DEEPMELLO:
Interviews with Anne-Christin Bansleben, 09.04.14, 26.05.14 + 09.07.15, Berlin

M.PATMOS:
Email interview with Marcia Patmos, 11.08.15
Sue Williamson, "M.Patmos Goes Global: Marcia Patmos talks about her International Woolmark Prize," *W Magazine*, 18.03.15, www.wmagazine.com/fashion/2015/03/m-patmos-goes-global/photos/

AIAYU:
Skype interview with Maria Høgh Heilmann, 22.05.15

LEMLEM:
Telephone interview with Liya Kebede, 10.09.15
Liya Kebede, "Approach Africa with a New Mindset," *Business of Fashion*, 13.05.15, www.businessoffashion.com/community/voices/discussions/what-will-it-take-for-africa-to-join-the-global-fashion-system/op-ed-approach-africa-with-a-new-mindset

FOLKDAYS:
Interviews with Lisa Jaspers, 13.11.13 + 27.06.15, Berlin

JUNGLE FOLK:
Skype interview with Pauline Maria Treis, 19.05.15
AL(MSS), "Treis, Pauline Marie, Zurich," Ma Petite Entreprise.ch, 03.12.13, www.ma-petite-entreprise.ch/portraits-dentrepreneurs/treis-pauline-marie-zurich

MICHAEL BRAUNGART + FRIEDERIKE VON WEDEL-PARLOW:
Interview with Michael Braungart + Friederike von Wedel-Parlow, 17.07.15, Berlin
Michael Braungart + William McDonough, *Cradle to Cradle: Remaking the Way We Make Things*, New York: North Point Press, 2002

MUD JEANS:
Interviews with Bert Van Son, 10.07.14 + 09.07.15, Berlin
"Moving towards a circular economy," European Commission/Environment, www.ec.europa.eu/environment/circular-economy/?cookies=disabled

PUYA:
Telephone interview with Timo Perschke, 20.08.13

PATAGONIA:
Telephone interview with Rick Ridgeway, 23.06.15
Tim Nudd, "Ad of the Day: Patagonia. The brand declares war on consumerism gone berserk, and admits its own environmental failings," *Adweek*, 28.11.11, www.adweek.com/news/advertising-branding/ad-day-patagonia-136745

J. B. Mackinnon, "Patagonia's Anti-Growth Strategy," *The New Yorker*, 21.05.15, www.newyorker.com/business/currency/patagonias-anti-growth-strategy

CHRISTOPHER RÆBURN:
Interview with Christopher Ræburn, 05.06.15, London
Fiona Sibley, "Christopher Ræburn: From parachute poncho to catwalk couture," *The Guardian*, 28.04.09, www.theguardian.com/lifeandstyle/2009/apr/28/christopher-raeburn
Sarah Mower, "Why London is Fast Becoming an Epicenter for Sustainable Fashion," *Vogue*, 31.10.14, www.vogue.com/3620949/kering-partners-with-centre-for-sustainable-fashion-london-college/

KNOWLEDGECOTTON APPAREL:
Telephone interview with Mads Mørup, 25.09.15

FREITAG:
Interview with Daniel + Markus Freitag, 29.08.15, Zurich

KINGS OF INDIGO:
Skype interview with Tony Tonnaer, 19.05.15

LIVING BLUE:
Skype interview with Mishael Aziz Ahmad, 24.04.15
"Living Blue: Best of Bangladesh," CARE, 30.09.13, www.care.org/work/economic-development/markets/living-blue-best-bangladesh
Anowarul Haq, "Self-owned social enterprise," *The Daily Star*, 17.10.12, http://archive.thedailystar.net/newDesign/news-details.php?nid=254055%253E%253E

REET AUS:
Interview with Reet Aus, 09.07.14, Berlin
Reet Aus, "Trash to Trend: Using Upcycling in Fashion Design," PhD diss., Estonian Academy of Arts, Tallinn, 2011

ORSOLA DE CASTRO + FASHION REVOLUTION:
Telephone interview with Orsola de Castro, 31.08.15
Caroline Howard, "On Fashion Revolution Day, Ask The Important Question: Who Made My Clothes?," *Forbes*, 24.04.15, www.forbes.com/sites/work-in-progress/2015/04/24/on-fashion-revolution-day-ask-the-important-question-who-made-my-clothes/

HESSNATUR:
Telephone interview with Marc Sommer + Marina Chahboune, 11.08.15

COCCCON:
Interview with Chandra Prakash Jha, 19.01.15, Berlin

PEOPLE TREE:
Interview with Safia Minney, 08.07.14, Berlin

LANIUS:
Telephone interview with Claudia Lanius, 20.02.15
"Eine Win-win-win-Situation," *bioRe® magazin*, Spring 2015, www.remei.ch/fileadmin/bioRe_Magazin_01_15.pdf
Ulrike Ascheberg-Klever, "Die Grüne Kusine," *Business: Handel*, 28.06.15, www.business-handel.de/unternehmergespraech/7817-green-f

UMASAN:
Interview with Anja + Sandra Umann, 28.01.15, Berlin

LILY COLE:
Email interview with Lily Cole, 13.08.15

8 EDEN AVENUE:
Telephone interview with Jessica Gruner, 28.05.15

JOHANNA RIPLINGER:
Telephone interview with Johanna Riplinger, 13.08.15

ALINASCHUERFELD:
Telephone interview with Alina Schürfeld, 07.05.15

TITANIA INGLIS:
Skype interview with Titania Inglis, 02.07.15
Ashley Garner, "Interview: Titania Inglis – Designing with Awareness. In studio with New York's coolest sustainable fashion designer," *Beautiful Savage*, 01.05.15, www.beautifulsavage.com/fashion/interview-titania-inglis-designing-awareness/

GLOSSARY:
Eco-Textile Labelling Guide, Pontefract: MCL Global, 2014
www.ecotextilelabels.com

PHOTO CREDITS

Cover: Design: maxjenny!, photo: Alexander Ilic, styling: Amanda Hörlin, hair/makeup: Mette Schou Agentur Cph, model: Flora, Le Management; back cover: top left: see p. 92; top right: see p. 106; bottom: see p. 182; p. 2: Niklas Hoejlund Photography, styling: Mette Krodsgaard wowstyling; p. 4: © Courtesy of Vivienne Westwood; p. 6: Julia Comita for Titania Inglis; p. 9: AIAYU, www.aiayu.com; pp. 10, 12, 13: Photography: Katia Wik, hair & makeup: Sarah Marx, model: Romina/Modelwerk; pp. 14, 15: Photography: Joachim Baldauf, styling: Claudia Hofman, hair & makeup: Sarah Marx; p. 16: Photographer: Kim Buckart; p. 17: Courtesy of Hellen van Rees; pp. 18, 19: Hellen van Rees; p. 20: Charlotte Abramow; pp. 21, 27: Courtesy of Honest by; p. 22 left: Frederik Heyman; pp. 22 right, 23, 24, 25: Alex Salinas; p. 30: Photo: Janette Gloor, hair & make-up: Anna Kalashnikova, clothes: Johanna Riplinger, model: Polina/Scout; pp. 32, 33: Photo: Ellin Anderegg, styling: Susi Bauer, hair & makeup: Melanie Volkart, hats: Silvio Hauke, model: Taly Fisch; pp. 34, 35: Photo: Ellin Anderegg, hair & makeup: Nina Tatavitto, styling: Jana Keller, clothes: Johanna Riplinger/stylists own, model: Veronika Kunz/Ooption; pp. 36, 38, 39, 40, 41: Photo: David Jagersma; p. 37: Photo: Ivonne Zijp; pp. 42–47: © Kowtow; pp. 48–51: Photo: Niklas Hoejlund Photography, styling: Mette Krodsgaard wowstyling; p. 52: Getty Images/Tristan Fewings; p. 53: Andy Gotts; pp. 54, 55, 56/57: © Courtesy of Vivienne Westwood; p. 59: Lea Crespi; pp. 62, 66, 67: Olivia Malone; pp. 63, 64, 65: Courtesy of Reformation; p. 68: Art direction & production: Modi Al Khufash, photography: harling & darsell, model: Vanessa Walther | Model Management, hair & makeup: Anja Fichtenmayer, typesetting & graphic design: DESIGN PER INCH; p. 69: Andreas Troitsch; pp. 72–75: Daniel McMahon; pp. 76–81: AIAYU, www.aiayu.com; p. 82: Patrick Desbrosses; p. 83: Kirsten Becken; p. 84: Ute Klein; p. 85: Patrick Desbrosses; pp. 86, 87, 88, 90/91: © lemlem; p. 89: Cameron Krone; pp. 92, 94–97: Campaign photo by Felipe Cuartas & Tomás Uribe; pp. 98–101: Daniel Breidt; pp. 106–109: © Mud Jeans; pp. 110–113: © Pyua; pp. 114–119: © Christopher Raeburn; pp. 120–123: Photos courtesy of Patagonia; pp. 124, 126,127, 128: Pascal Grob; p. 125: Roland Taennler; p. 129 top, bottom left: Oliver Nanz; p. 129 bottom right: Yves Bachmann; pp. 130–133: © Knowledge Cotton; pp. 134–137: © KINGS OF INDIGO; p. 138: Bianca Chainal; p. 139, 140/141: Living Blue/Paul David Barikder; p. 143: Tamzin Haughton; pp. 144, 146, 147: Herkki Erich Merila; p. 145: Andrei Chertkov; pp. 148–153: © Hess Natur-Textilien GmbH; pp. 154–157: © People Tree; pp. 158, 160, 161: Heike Wippermann; pp. 162, 164, 165: LANIUS natwear GmbH, photographer: Marcus Gloger; p. 163: Fabian Stuertz; pp. 166–171: Copyright: A&S Umann GmbH; p. 173: Emir Eralp; pp. 174–177: www.johannariplinger.com, Photo: Sarah Dulay, Luisa F. c/o East West Models; pp. 178, 180, 181: Photography: Daniele Glunz/www.dglunz.de; p. 179: Weyer + Grill Studios; pp. 182, 184, 185: Julia Comita for Titania Inglis; p. 183: Eric Morales

© Prestel Verlag, Munich · London · New York, 2016

A member of Verlagsgruppe Random House GmbH
Neumarkter Strasse 28 · 81673 Munich

Prestel Publishing Ltd.
14–17 Wells Street
London W1T 3PD

Prestel Publishing
900 Broadway, Suite 603
New York, NY 10003

Cover: maxjenny!, Autumn/Winter 2016
Back cover: Junglefolk, Moon Safari, Autumn/
Winter 2014/15 (top left); Mud Jeans, Autumn/
Winter 2015/16 (top right); Titania Inglis,
Autumn/Winter 2015/16 (bottom)
P. 2: maxjenny!, Sub Culture;
p. 4: Vivienne Westwood, Gold Label,
Spring/Summer 2013;
p. 6: Titania Inglis,
Autumn/Winter 2015/16;
p. 9: Aiayu, Wear,
Autumn/Winter 2015/16

Library of Congress Control Number: 2016931162; British Library Cataloguing-in-Publication Data: a catalogue record for this book is available from the British Library.

In respect to links in the book, the Publisher expressly notes that no illegal content was discernible on the linked sites at the time the links were created. The Publisher has no influence at all over the current and future design, content or authorship of the linked sites. For this reason the Publisher expressly disassociates itself from all content on linked sites that has been altered since the link was created and assumes no liability for such content.

Editorial direction: Julie Kiefer
Editorial assistance: Adeline Henzschel
Translation: Jane Michael
Copyediting: Jonathan Fox
Picture editing: Magdalena Schaffrin & Ellen Köhrer; Andrea Weißenbach
Design and layout: Paul Sloman / +SUBTRACT
Production: Friederike Schirge
Origination: Reproline Genceller
Printing and binding: DZS Grafik, d.o.o., Ljubljana

Printed in Slovenia

FSC
www.fsc.org
MIX
Paper from
responsible sources
FSC® C110418

Verlagsgruppe Random House FSC® N001967
Printed on the FSC®-certified paper Tauro

ISBN 978-3-7913-8176-3

www.prestel.com